Quotations of James Monroe

Table of Contents

Foreword 3
Illustrations 7
Introduction 9
Chronology 11
Characters 15
Monroe on Family & Friends 19
    Elizabeth Kortright Monroe 19
    Eliza Monroe Hay 20
    Maria Monroe Gouverneur 20
    James Spence Monroe 22
    Father's Role 23
    Joseph Jones Monroe 23
    Andrew Monroe 24
    James Monroe, Jr. 25
    Spence & Elizabeth Jones Monroe 26
    Joseph Jones 26
    Thomas Jefferson 27
    James Madison 29
    Jefferson and Madison 29
    George Washington 30
    John Quincy Adams 31
    Marquis de Lafayette & Madame Lafayette 31
    William Short 32
    George Mason 33
    Oliver Hazard Perry 33
Monroe on Private Affairs 34
    His Education 34
    His Bad Handwriting 35
    Romance 35
    Religion 36

- Farms & Farming 37
- Ash Lawn-Highland 38
- Retirement 39

Monroe on Public Affairs 51
- American Revolution 51
- Civic Virtue 53
- Government 55
- Slavery 57
- Education 59
- Defense 62
- Indians 63
- The Presidency 65
- The Federalists 66
- Louisiana 66
- Great Britain 67
- War of 1812 67
- Missouri Compromise 69
- Greece 69
- Spanish American Independence 70
- Monroe Doctrine 71

On the Monroes 72
- James Monroe 72
- Criticism of Monroe 81
- Elizabeth Kortright Monroe 83
- Eliza Monroe Hay 85
- Maria Monroe Gouverneur 86

Death of James Monroe 88

National Honors for Monroe 89

Index 91

Quotations of James Monroe
on the Subjects of
His Family, Friends, Private Affairs,
and Public Policy

To Which is Appended

On the Monroes:
A Sampler of Quotations from
Assorted Personages on
James Monroe and His Family

With

A Selection of Portraits and Views

Compiled by
Daniel Preston and Heidi Stello

Copyright © 2010 by Ash Lawn-Highland

Design and layout by The Thompson Group,
   Fredericksburg, VA, USA

Printed by BMS Direct, Inc.
   Lynchburg, VA, USA

First Edition: March 2010
   10 9 8 7 6 5 4 3 2 1

ISBN: 978-1-4507-0862-3

Published by Ash Lawn-Highland, the home of James Monroe, Charlottesville, Virginia. Ash Lawn-Highland is an historic property of the College of William & Mary, Williamsburg, Virginia.

Cover photo: James Monroe by Charles Bird King
Loudoun County Court House, Leesburg, VA

Foreword

In 1992 Paula Xinis-Fishman of Ash Lawn-Highland assembled a collection of quotations by and about James Monroe and his family in a booklet entitled *Monroe On....* When the last copy of Paula's book sold, we turned to Daniel Preston and Heidi Stello at the Papers of James Monroe at the University of Mary Washington and asked them to compile a new edition, with the title of *Quotations of James Monroe*. They readily accepted, and prepared this revised and greatly expanded edition of the original. We are very pleased with the result and are most happy to make this book available once again.

Carolyn C. Holmes
Executive Director
Ash Lawn-Highland

Illustrations

James Monroe (Gilbert Stuart) 42

James Monroe (Samuel F. B. Morse) 43

Elizabeth Monroe (Louis Sené) 44

Elizabeth Monroe (Raphaelle Peale) 44

Elizabeth Monroe (Frances Maury Burke) 45

Eliza Monroe (unknown artist) 46

Maria Monroe (Pietro Cardelli) 46

Eliza Monroe Hay (S. Canuson) 47

George Hay (Cephas Thompson) 47

Maria Monroe Gouverneur (Charles Bird King) 48

Samuel Lawrence Gouverneur 48

Joseph J. Monroe (attributed to Ezra Ames) 49

Andrew Monroe (unknown artist) 49

Highland 50

Highland 50

Introduction

James Monroe, the fifth president of the United States, had a long and distinguished public career lasting over fifty-five years—beginning with his service in the Continental army at age seventeen in 1776 and lasting until his death on July 4, 1831. During that time he wrote thousands of letters, speeches, and essays in which he commented on the great events and issues of his time, including the American Revolution, slavery, and the role of government. He offered remarks on family members and on friends—notably Thomas Jefferson, George Washington, and James Madison—and on matters of common concern, such as education and religion.

In our current age of speech writers, press secretaries, and media specialists, we are accustomed to public figures making speeches with built-in applause points and featuring sound bites—those short and pithy statements designed to be presented in ten-second spots in news broadcasts. During Monroe's era, statesmen developed their ideas in longer expositions without a thought of single sentences or phrases being excerpted to summarize their points. Monroe (and others of his age) did occasionally offer short, quotable remarks, and many are included in this collection. But just as frequently it has been necessary to quote entire paragraphs in order to grasp the fullness of Monroe's ideas.

A large collection of Monroe's correspondence and papers survives, but it is, to a great extent, related primarily to public affairs. Monroe tried to keep his private life separate from his public career, and according to family tradition he destroyed his family correspondence before he died. Some private letters do exist, but they are comparatively few in number (only one letter from him to his wife still exists, and only a handful of correspondence between Monroe and his children and other family members survives). As a result, there is a great wealth of material on Monroe's public life, but very little of his writing comments on family matters or his private affairs. The family letters that do survive are incredibly rich in their content and make us wish that we had more.

Given Monroe's long public career, there are, of course, many descriptions of him written by his friends and associates. The second section of this book is a collection of quotations from his contemporaries describing Monroe, his wife, and his daughters. Although they do not express Monroe's ideas on matters of concern to him, these quotes do illuminate his personality and give us an idea of what his contemporaries thought of him and his family. As such, we thought that they would make a useful addition to the book.

An earlier version of this book, compiled by Paula Xinis-Fishman and entitled *Monroe On*, was published by Ash Lawn-Highland in 1992. The booklet proved very popular and has sold out. This new edition expands upon and replaces the previous one. The current version is, for the most part, a new book and not a revision, but Ms. Xinis-Fishman's compilation served as a starting point, and we wish to acknowledge her contribution.

Chronology of the Life of James Monroe

28 April 1758	born in Westmoreland County, Virginia
June 1774	began studies at College of William and Mary
February 1776	commissioned lieutenant in the Continental army
26 December 1776	wounded at Battle of Trenton
January-June 1778	at Valley Forge
20 December 1778	resigned from the Continental army at rank of major
15 August 1779	appointed lieutenant-colonel in the Virginia service
January 1780	began to study law with Thomas Jefferson
April-June 1782	member of the Virginia House of Delegates
June 1782	admitted to bar
1782-1783	member of the Council of State of Virginia
1783-1786	delegate to the Continental Congress
16 February 1786	married Elizabeth Kortright in New York City
October 1786	established residence in Fredericksburg, VA opened law office
December 1786	Eliza Monroe (daughter) born

Quotations of James Monroe

1787-1789	member of the Virginia House of Delegates
2-27 June 1788	member of Virginia convention for ratification of the U. S. Constitution
1790-1793	member of the U. S. Senate
1793	purchased farm in Albemarle County, VA (Ash Lawn-Highland)
1794-1797	U. S. minister to France
May 1799	James Spence Monroe (son) born
1799-1802	governor of Virginia
28 September 1800	James Spence Monroe died
April 1802	Maria Hester Monroe (daughter) born
1803	special envoy to France—signed Louisiana Purchase treaty
1803-1807	U. S. minister to Great Britain
1805	special envoy to Spain
1808	nominated as candidate for president by dissident Republicans
1810-1811	member of the Virginia House of Delegates
January-April 1811	governor of Virginia
1811-1817	secretary of state under President Madison
December 1812 - February 1813	acting secretary of war
August 1814- March 1815	secretary of war
4 March 1817	inaugurated as president
5 March 1821	inaugurated for second term as president

2 December 1823	enunciated Monroe Doctrine
25 March 1825	retired to his farm at Oak Hill in Loudoun County, VA
23 September 1830	Elizabeth Kortright Monroe died
October 1830	moved to New York City
4 July 1831	died in New York City

Characters

Elizabeth Kortright Monroe (1768-1830) was Monroe's wife. She was born in New York City and was the daughter of Lawrence Kortright, a merchant. She and Monroe married in New York on 16 February 1786 and moved to Virginia in October of that year. Elizabeth Monroe was a beautiful and elegant woman, but she was plagued throughout her life by poor health.

Eliza Monroe Hay (1786-1840) was Monroe's eldest child. She married **George Hay** (1765-1830), a prominent Virginia attorney and jurist, in 1808. They had one daughter, Hortensia.

James Spence Monroe (1799-1800), the Monroes' infant son and middle child, died at sixteen months of age.

Maria Monroe Gouverneur (1802-1850) was Monroe's youngest child. She married her cousin **Samuel Gouverneur** (1799-1867) in a ceremony at the White House in 1820. They resided in New York City.

Joseph Jones Monroe (1771-1824) was Monroe's youngest brother. He was by profession an attorney, but was never successful in the business. James Monroe's correspondence suggests that his brother drank and gambled too much, and he was constantly in debt.

Andrew Monroe (d. 1826) was Monroe's younger brother. He was a farmer who depended on his older brother for financial support.

James Monroe, Jr. (1799-1870) was Monroe's nephew, the son of Andrew Monroe. He attended the U. S. Military Academy, had a career in the army, and served one term in the House of

Representatives. He and his uncle were very close, and the elder Monroe treated him like a son.

Emily Monroe was a daughter of Joseph Jones Monroe.

Little is known about Monroe's parents. His father, **Spence Monroe** (d. 1774), was a planter, and he died when Monroe was sixteen. His mother, **Elizabeth Jones Monroe**, apparently died sometime between the birth of Joseph Jones Monroe in 1771 and the death of Spence Monroe in 1774. They had five children, of which James was the second.

Joseph Jones (1727-1805) was Monroe's uncle and, after the death of Monroe's father, his guardian. Jones was an important political figure in revolutionary Virginia and was Monroe's political patron and mentor.

Monroe's long friendship and political association with **Thomas Jefferson** began in 1780 when Monroe began to study law under Jefferson's direction.

Monroe first met **James Madison** in the early 1780s. The two men (and their families) were very close friends, but they were also, at times, political rivals, a situation that sometimes strained their friendship.

Monroe greatly admired **George Washington**, particularly for his leadership during the Revolutionary War. Political differences divided them during the 1790s, and each bitterly resented the other during the last years of Washington's life. Monroe abandoned his resentment after Washington's death, and in later years had nothing but praise for the general.

Monroe met **John Quincy Adams** in 1785, but they had only sporadic contact until 1811 when Monroe became secretary of state and Adams was serving as U. S. minister to Russia. Monroe's great respect for Adams' ability led him to appoint Adams as secretary of state in his cabinet. Both men were experienced and skilled diplomats, and they worked closely together in shaping American foreign policy.

Monroe and the **Marquis de Lafayette** served together during the Revolutionary War and remained close friends. The Monroes were instrumental in obtaining the release of **Madame Lafayette** from prison in Paris where she had been jailed during the French Revolution. In 1824 President Monroe arranged for Lafayette to make a visit to the United States.

Monroe became friends with **William Short** when they were students at the College of William and Mary; they later served together on the Virginia Council of State. Like Monroe, Short was a protégé of Jefferson. He owned a farm in Albemarle County next to Monroe's estate, but he never lived there, preferring to reside in Philadelphia.

George Mason was a key figure in revolutionary Virginia. He was a strong proponent of the inclusion of a bill of rights in the U. S. Constitution.

Oliver Hazard Perry had a long and distinguished career in the navy and achieved fame during the War of 1812 for his victory in the battle on Lake Erie. He died in 1816 while on a diplomatic mission to Venezuela.

Monroe on Family and Friends

Elizabeth Kortright Monroe

I find that my position here [in London] exposes me to greater expence than I had expected, so much as to preclude all hope of deriving any advantage from it.... The moisture of the climate and smoak, have given us all colds, & [Mrs. Monroe] is attended with a stricture of the breast, which is an additional reason for us to get home as soon as possible. *(Monroe to Joseph Jones, 12 March 1804)*

We are doomed to suffer much in this world, neither of us have escaped our afflictions, of a publick nature – but both have been happy in domestick life. *(Monroe to Charles F. Mercer, 18 November 1811)*

We hope also that Mrs. Campbell is pleased with her new residence. Mrs. M. may speak with approving conscience on this point, as she left her state & her family, & became a good Virginian. *(Monroe to George W. Campbell, 6 September 1815)*

I have left my family [in Washington] with extreme regret; your aunt's [Elizabeth Monroe] health is very precarious, & her head often much affected. Light circumstances overwhelm her. She requires indulgence and care. Her mind is fixed on her children, & grandchildren, and is always talking of them when we are alone. Maria's absence distresses her, as does the situation of Mrs. Hay, tho' to others she says little about it. My earnest wish is that you do all that you can to console her, without appearing to make it an object, and the same with respect to Eliza. *(Monroe to Samuel Gouverneur, 11 May 1823)*

I have decided to accompany Mrs. Monroe on a visit to Mr. Gouverneur and our daughter [Maria]. Her health will I think be benefitted by the journey, and afterwards, by the society of our family there, including our grandchildren. *(Monroe to Thomas Swann, 19 May 1828)*

We have both suffer'd, the most afflicting calamity that can befall us in this life, and which, if time may alleviate, it cannot efface. After having lived, with the partner of your cares, in so many vicissitudes of life, so long together, and afforded to each other, comforts, which no other person on earth can so do, as both of us have done, to have her snatched from us, is an affliction, which none but those who feel it, can justly estimate. I seldom leave the house. Never but when the weather permits me to take exercise in a carriage. *(Monroe to James Brown, 9 December 1830)*

Eliza Monroe Hay and Maria Monroe Gouverneur

Immediately on our arrival here we had [Eliza] inoculated. She had that disease [smallpox] very favorably and recovered from it. *(Monroe to Nicholas Lewis, 7 February 1791)*

Don't forget among all of your useful acquirements the comparatively trivial one of playing & singing several airs upon the harp. I will get one at Paris. That is an accomplishment that will be really useful to you. *(Monroe to Eliza Monroe, 1 March 1805)*

I have full confidence that your courage will never fail you in any trial, to which others of your sex have been found equal.... We miss you, my dear child much, but after a short time we flatter ourselves that our respective situation will be such, as to secure us the company of Mr. Hay and yourself and the young family which you may raise to him every summer. *(Monroe to Eliza Monroe Hay, 10 July 1809)*

Tell Eliza I am very anxious to be made acquainted with my young relation [Hortensia Hay]; that I hope she will take after her mother's family and not her father's. *(Monroe to George Hay, 24 September 1809)*

We have just received letters from Richmond by which we hear that Eliza, who has been much indisposed, is getting in better health. She inquired affectionately after you. Her child is a lovely babe & promises to be handsome. Eliza makes an excellent mother as she does a retired & domestick wife. Mrs. Monroe has been much indisposed with the rheumatism this winter but is now better. Maria has enjoyed tolerable good health. She is as sprightly & wild as when you were with us. *(Monroe to Elizabeth Trist, 6 March 1810)*

Mr. Taylor, a respectable and intelligent clergyman, takes Maria, and says that he had rather receive her as she is, than when further advanced. I trust that she will progress rapidly under his tuition. *(George Hay to Monroe, 9 October 1812)*

My family is now in Virginia. Our two daughters are the delight and consolation, with a granddaughter, of their mother's and my own life. They are everything to us which we could desire. They have never given a moment of pain by their conduct. Mrs. Hay, whom you know to be remarkably gay and lively, when a girl, is now a retired, sedate and diligent domestic character, delighted only with her own family and the society of her mother and sister. Maria, now in her 11th year, delicate in her health on her return home, begins to recover from the effect of our climate and to gain strength, is at her age like her sister at the present one, with the best disposition possible. *(Monroe to Fulwar Skipwith, 12 August 1813)*

Tell Eliza that Maria talks much of her & Hortensia; that she is a most excellent child, without fault that we discern, and with the best qualities. She is apt at school, and getting forward in reading writing & drawing. *(Monroe to George Hay, 12 January 1815)*

Our youngest daughter Maria, is at school in Philadelphia, much grown of late & finishing her education in the spring, with Madame Greland, a French lady of merit. *(Monroe to Fulwar Skipwith, 28 November 1818)*

Take care of your children who are dear to us, as well as to you and Samuel. Our affectionate regards to you all, & to the whole connection to whom we are much attached. *(Monroe to Maria Gouverneur, 6 June 1830)*

James Spence Monroe

We have it is true added to our family a son, now twelve months old, a fine boy who runs about, begins to talk a few words, & is highly interesting to us. I was balancing for some time what I should call him, and among the worthies of our country can assure you, had his mother come into the idea of calling him after one, I should have thought more of the names of Jefferson & Montgomery than any we boast of. But his mother is an old fashioned woman & chose, without regarding any consideration of that kind, to follow the old fashioned track of calling him after his father, which will be done as soon as she moves home where she expects to have that office performed by the clergyman who baptized his sister. *(Monroe to Janet Montgomery, 6 May 1800)*

An unhappy event has occurr'd which has overwhelmed us with grief. At ten last night our beloved babe departed this life after several days sickness, which attended the cuting his eye teeth in the last stage, when we flatter'd ourselves the danger had passed. I cannot give you an idea of the effect this event has produc'd on my family, or of my own affliction in being a partner and spectator of the scene. Many things have occur'd my friend, in these late years that abated my sensibility to the affairs of this world, but this has roused me beyond what I thought it was possible I could be. Knowing the interest you take in our welfare, I perform a painful task in communicating to you and family this great calamity. *(Monroe to James Madison, 29 September 1800)*

I wish the grave of our infant son in the church yard at Richmond to be noted by something more permanent than the memory of our estimable friends who tend his deposit there. A small stone at his head with the inscription of his name will be sufficient, 'J. S. M.' *(Monroe to Joseph Jones, 2 March 1803)*

A Father's Role

A father is the natural guardian & protector of his children. When they separate, there must be great cause for it, and the explanation always a painful circumstance, if not an injurious one to him. *(Monroe to Emily Monroe, 24 July 1812)*

Joseph Jones Monroe

He has been in Scotland since 1783 & is now in his 19th year. His acquirments in the classics are respectable. In the line of philosophy, history &c less so, owing to his having been depriv'd of the admonition of a friend, who had return'd to this country, when it became of the most importance. In this stage his youthful propensities for gaiety & society, gain'd the ascendency over his prudence, & took him in a great measure from his studies, & led him into some expences that were improper, & which he has sincerely lament'd. He is now with me reading the law & applies to it with great assiduity. I think his genius equal to any thing he may undertake & I have no doubt of the necessary exertions on his part for the future. *(Monroe to Thomas Jefferson, 16 January 1790)*

I recollect there is a billiard table near you; let me warn you against it. A passion of this kind will controul as it always has every other. If it seizes you, your clients money will not be safe in your hands. *(Monroe to Joseph J. Monroe, 16 June 1794)*

I am aware, that for your father to take his family with him to Natchez, and to succeed there, would require self-command on his part, perfect sobriety, steady attention to business, economy, selection of his company, & in fact that kind of conduct, which every prudent man would observe, wherever he might be. Whether he is capable of observing this kind of conduct, after the experience he has had, which must convince him, that without it, his ruin is inevitable, I know not. You, and your sister and Mr. Cabell, who know his habits, and have weighed every circumstance, can better determine the question than me, who know but little of him, for you will recollect that I have never had much intercourse or communication with him. He always declined it. *(Monroe to Emily Monroe, 24 July 1812)*

I think proper to state that when your father left Albemarle before, & mov'd to Tappahannock he left his debts unpaid. I was told that he was thriving in business there, and that if I aided him then & paid those debts, it would make his fortune and that of his family, while if his creditors followed him, he would be ruined. I was told also that it would be the last call he would ever make on me. I relieved him from those debts amounting to at least £400. That was in 1798. The next year I moved to Richmond, and immediately at my arrival there, he drew on me for £80 to save him from failures he said. I paid it, tho I was in great distress at the time. About two years afterwards, when your mother was on her death bed, he was again distressed by creditors, and your uncle Andrew wrote me that if I did not interpose, the bed would be taken from under her by executions in the hands of the sheriff. He said that his debts amounted to about £300, and that the sheriff would take my engagement for them. I gave it, and the debts amounted to upward of £400 which I paid. For the balance of his debts in Scotland, I paid about the same time, to Mr. Patten in Fredericksburg, that is, in 1801, and upwards of £600 and while I was in England in 1806 I paid to Sir Wm Forbes, another balance of about £200. Since his return to Albemarle, I have made the advances, which I have already stated, without taking into the account, many smaller advances, and suppers he has had at my house since I left home. *(Monroe to Emily Monroe, 24 July 1812)*

Andrew Monroe

He is an honest good hearted man, but advancing in years, and in a great measure helpless. When I sell out in Loudoun, I do not know where he will go. He don't appear to me to have any fixed plan and I presume expects aid from me. I have twice before saved him from ruin.... *(Monroe to James Monroe, Jr., 9 May 1814)*

James Monroe, Jr.

You have books, can have assistance, when you want it, and may every day improve yourself. Among other studies, should be that of the French language. In short I would take advantage of the opportunity to improve yourself, in every useful study. (Monroe to James Monroe, Jr., 24 December 1813)

The character which a young man gets [at the military academy], will remain to him through life. Try therefore to establish a good one. The way to do it, is plain, and obvious. Apply closely to your studies, improve, and enlarge your understanding. Study first, those branches of science that belong to your profession, mathematicks in various branches... Study also history, of different countries, England, France, the U States, and of other nations. Study the history of Rome, and Greece, which is called antient history.... Chronology ought to be attended to, that is, the account of time.... You may be satisfied that if you are idle, and neglect the opportunity you now have, to improve yourself, all future prospect of success will be [lost]. But that if you are industrious, will study close, behave well, acquire considerable knowledge and a good character you may do well. (Monroe to James Monroe, Jr., 9 May 1814)

Your education, in more early life, having been neglected, subjects you to disadvantages, which you must sensibly feel. There is no way of getting the better of these, than by close study for a year or two, for one at least, and that may be better pursued at the academy, than at a garrison or other place. There you will learn many things besides your profession. . . . What you may be hereafter, will depend on your exertions now. Your present defects, will be attributed to your youth, and allowances be made for them. But soon your character, will be fixed, and unless, you improve yourself, much, you will not be so much thought of as you might be. (Monroe to James Monroe, Jr., 25 November 1816)

I thought it proper to give you advice as to every step you took, to prevent your falling into error, and making blunders, which an inexperienced youth would be apt to do, to his great misfortune, if not his ruin. Indeed, too many are ruined by indiscreet and improper conduct, in their first beginning owing to the want of such advice. I will now state wherein you neglected to take my advice but hope not much if any to your injury. I do it not to reproach you with it, but merely to put you on your guard as to the future. If you have been mistaken, as to the past, in any instance, there is no reason why you should be in the future. And if my advice is of any service to you, I shall be glad to hear it. (Monroe to James Monroe, Jr., 25 November 1816)

I find that you hardly ever went near them [Monroe's friends in New York], accepted invitations, which you did not comply with, keeping them from dinner, waiting for you. That you kept at the coffee house, or tavern, in very low company, such as it was, at times, improper to be seen in. That you called for wine, when called on, and expended money improperly, even if your own, and the more so, if borrowed. . . . I have stated these things, to guard you against error, as to the future. I hope the account of the past is more unfavorable than you deserve. So much the better. Try to avoid error, and to do in all things, what is right. This is all I wish of you. It is for your advantage to do so, and I am your friend in advising it. You are your own enemy, if you do not follow the advice. (*Monroe to James Monroe Jr., 25 November 1816*)

Spence and Elizabeth Jones Monroe

His father, Spence Monroe...was a very worthy and respectable citizen possessed of good landed and other property. His mother, Elizabeth Jones, was a very amiable and respectable woman, possessing the best domestic qualities, a good wife and good parent. (*Autobiography of James Monroe*)

Joseph Jones

I have just heard of the death of our estimable and venerable friend Mr. Jones. This event has afflicted us in the manner it was natural it should do, as he held the place and was always regarded by my family as a parent. We hoped to have found him in good health on our return, and it was a part of our common plan in which we were greatly interested, that he should have passed his declining years under our care. It is consoling to know that he died in Fredericksburg where he would receive all the aid and attention which medical skill and friendship could furnish. *(Monroe to James Madison, 10 January 1806)*

Thomas Jefferson

A variety of disappointments with respect to the prospects of my private fortune… which failed in a manner which could not have been expected, perplexed my plan of life & exposed me to inconveniences which had nearly destroyed me. In this situation had I not formed a connection with you I should most certainly have retired from society with a resolution never to have entered on the stage again. *(Monroe to Thomas Jefferson, 9 September 1780)*

In this situation you became acquainted with me, and undertook the direction of my studies; and, believe me, I feel that what I am at present in the opinion of others, or whatever I may be in the future, has greatly arisen from your friendship. *(Monroe to Thomas Jefferson, 9 September 1780)*

I have not relinquished the prospect of being your neighbor. The house for which I have requested a plan may possibly be erected near Monticello—to fix there and to have yourself in particular, with what friends we may collect around for society is my chief object, or rather the only one which promises to me, in this connection I have formed real and substantial pleasure. *(Monroe to Thomas Jefferson, 19 August 1786)*

Whether to move up immediately or hereafter, when I shall be so happy to have you for a neighbor I have not determined. In any event, it puts it within my reach to be contiguous to you when the fatigue of public life sho'd dispose you for retirement, and in the interim will enable me, in respect to your affairs, as I shall be frequently in Charlottesville, as a summer retreat in attendance on the district court there, to render you some service. *(Monroe to Thomas Jefferson, 15 February 1789)*

I have no hesitation to declare, that I consider the late election to the Executive of the United States, as having essentially contributed to secure to us the enjoyment of the blessings for which we contended in our revolution. *(Annual message to the Virginia General Assembly, 7 December 1801)*

... for from the high respect which I have entertained for your publick service, talents & virtues I have seen the national interest, and your advancement and fame so intimately connected, as to constitute essentially the same cause. Besides I have never forgotten the proofs of kindness & friendship which I have received from you in early life.... [Y]ou may be assured that I shall never cease to take a deep interest in your political fame & personal happiness. *(Monroe to Thomas Jefferson, 27 February 1808)*

To do you any injury, or indeed anyone in the administration never entered into my mind, for while I labour'd under a conviction not only that I had been injur'd but that the friendly feeling which you had so long entertain'd for me, had ceased to exist, I never indulg'd any other sentiment in consequence of it, than that of sorrow. At present I am happy to say, that doubt of your friendship for me, having experienced any change is completely done away, and that the only anxiety, which I feel, is to satisfy you, that the impression was not taken on slight ground, nor imputable to communications made me by persons out of the administration. *(Monroe to Thomas Jefferson, 22 March 1808)*

The late calamity with which you have been afflicted by the loss of your most estimable father, my friend, has given me the most heartfelt concern. Having been connected by the closest ties of friendship, with both your parents, from my earliest youth, I have always cherished the sentiments, with which I was animated at that period, with great interest, & have witnessed the late occurrence, with the deepest regret. *(Monroe to Martha Jefferson Randolph, 16 July 1826)*

I thank you for your kindness in sending me a copy of your oration, on the death of Mr. Jefferson, which I have read with great interest & satisfaction.... Having studied the law under him in my youth, and been long engaged in the same career of public service since, I have known his great integrity, patriotism & important services. It is very gratifying to me to see a just tribute of respect paid to his memory. *(Monroe to John Tyler, 13 August 1826)*

James Madison

No one knows better than I do the merit of Mr. Madison, and I can declare that should he be elected he will have my best wishes for the success of his administration, as well on account of the great interest which I take in what concerns his welfare as in that of my country. *(Monroe to Thomas Jefferson, 27 February 1808)*

Of my immediate predecessor, under whom so important a portion of this great and successful experiment has been made, I shall be pardoned for expressing my earnest wishes that he may long enjoy in his retirement the affections of a grateful country, the best reward of exalted talents and the most faithful and meritorious services. *(First inaugural address, 4 March 1817)*

My ill state of health continuing... renders the restoration of my health very uncertain or indeed any favorable change in it.... I deeply regret that there is no prospect of our ever meeting again, since so long have we been connected... that a final separation is among the most distressing incidents which could occur. *(Monroe to James Madison, 11 April 1831)*

Jefferson and Madison

... it is my candid opinion, that Mr. Jefferson and Mr. Madison have done more, since the establishment of the revolution (in which Gen. W. was preeminent) than any two persons on the continent. *(Monroe to George Hay, 2 May 1819)*

In the example of my illustrious predecessors, I see a conclusive proof of the success and stability of our republican institutions. In their lives, we read the great events of a nation, struggling for, and maintaining its independence. Our whole Union bears unequivocal testimony to their extraordinary services, and very exalted merit. *(Speech, Savannah, Georgia, 10 May 1819)*

George Washington

The conduct of Gen. Washington [during the adoption of the Constitution] has no doubt been right and meritorious. All parties had acknowledged defects in the federal system, and been sensible of the propriety of some material change. To forsake the honourable retreat to which he had retired & risque the reputation he had so deservedly acquir'd, manifested a zeal for the publick interest, that could after so many and illustrious services, & at this stage of life, scarcely have been expected from him. Having however commenc'd again on the publick theatre the course which he takes becomes not only highly interesting to him but likewise so to us: the human character is not perfect; and if he partakes of those qualities which we have too much reason to believe are almost inseparable from the frail nature of our being, the people of America will perhaps be lost: be assured his influence carried this government; for my own part I have a boundless confidence in him nor have I any reason to believe he will ever furnish occasion for withdrawing it. More is to be apprehended if he takes a part in the public councils again as he advances in age from the designs of those around him than from any dispositions of his own. *(Monroe to Thomas Jefferson, 12 July 1788)*

On the 15th of June, 1775 a commander in chief of the forces raised and to be raised for the defense of American liberty was appointed by the unanimous vote of Congress, and his conduct in the discharge of the duties of that high trust, which he held through the whole of the war, has given an example to the world for talents as a military commander; for integrity, fortitude, and firmness under the severest trials; for respect to the civil authority and devotion to the rights and liberties of his country, of which neither Rome nor Greece have exhibited the equal. I saw him in my earliest youth, in the retreat through Jersey, at the head of a small band, or rather, in its rear, for he was always near the enemy, and his countenance and manner made an impression on me which time can never efface.... A deportment so firm, so dignified, so exalted, but yet so modest and composed, I have never seen in any other person. *(Message to Congress, 4 May 1822)*

I never doubted the perfect integrity of Gen. Washington, nor the strength, or energy of his mind, and was personally attached to him. I admired his patriotism, and had full confidence in his attachment to liberty, and solicitude for the success of the French revolution. *(Monroe to John McLean, 5 December 1827)*

John Quincy Adams

Respect for your talents and patriotic services has induced me to commit to your care, with the sanction of the Senate, the Department of State. I have done this in confidence that it will be agreeable to you to accept it, which I can assure you will be very gratifying to me. *(Monroe to John Quincy Adams, 6 March 1817)*

In your friendship I have the most perfect confidence, having seen in your conduct, while I was in the Administration, and since my retirement, the most uniform & satisfactory proofs of it.... I shall always be happy to see you here, & take a sincere & great interest in your welfare & happiness. *(Monroe to John Quincy Adams, 17 December 1828)*

Marquis de Lafayette and Madame Lafayette

In this carriage Mrs. Monroe drove directly to the prison in which Madame Lafayette was confined. As soon as it entered the street, the public attention was drawn to it, and at the prison gate the crowd gathered around it.... On hearing that the wife of the American minister had called on the most friendly motives to see her, she became frantic, and in that state, they met.... [T]he liberation of Madame Lafayette soon followed, on which event she hastened directly to his house, where she was received with warmest affection. *(Autobiography of James Monroe)*

In conformity with a resolution of Congress of the last session, an invitation was given to General Lafayette to visit the United States.... In August last he arrived at New York, where he was received with the warmth of affection and gratitude to which his very important and disinterested services and sacrifices in our Revolutionary struggle so eminently entitled him.... It is natural that we should all take a deep interest in his future welfare, as we do. His high claims on our Union are felt, and the sentiment universal that they should be met in a generous spirit. Under these impressions I invite your attention to the subject, with a view that, regarding his very important services, losses, and sacrifices, a provision may be made and tendered to him which shall correspond with the sentiments and be worthy the character of the American people. *(Annual message to Congress, 7 December 1824)*

If I was ever to visit France your house would be my home, but we are both too far advanced in years to think of such a voyage... I do not know that anything will appear to the public during my life, but whenever it does... a just regard will be shewn to your services, and claims on our countries, as well as to the friendly relation which has existed between us and our families. *(Monroe to Lafayette, 2 May 1829)*

William Short

You expressed a desire to sell your land near me. Cannot you come & reside on it? If you cannot prevail on a Lady from one of our great cities to bury herself there with you, one might be found in the neighborhood, of merit & worth, to whom the solitude would not be irksome. If you ever intend to make such an arrangement, you ought not to postpone it much longer. I am now 51 years of age; you are I presume not more than 10 years younger. In 1795 when we were in Paris together you were about

5 years younger. In 1775 when we were at College, the difference between us was still less. I hope you will take this affair into consideration, & decide in favor of my counsel, & come & establish yourself near me ere long. *(Monroe to William Short, 16 February 1811)*

George Mason

You have before this I presume heard of the death of Col. George Mason which was about the 8th of this month of the gout in the stomack. His patriotic virtues thro the revolution will ever be remember'd by the citizens of this country, and his death at the present moment will be sensibly felt by the republican interest. *(Monroe to Thomas Jefferson, 16 October 1792)*

Oliver Hazard Perry

... [I]t is with deep regret I have to state the loss which has been sustained by the death of Commodore Perry. His gallantry in a brilliant exploit in the late war added to the renown of his country. His death is deplored as a national misfortune. *(Annual message to Congress, 7 December 1819)*

Monroe on Private Affairs

His Education

I am agreeably situated in my quarters & in my society. In the first instance I have private lodgings & live by myself; in the 2d I hardly ever leave them nor join society nor do I feel a disposition for it.... I have however the advantage of access to the College [of William & Mary] Library which forms the principal part of my amusement. *(Monroe to William Woodford, September 1779)*

Since my return from Richmond I have liv'd a very sedentary life upon a small estate I have in King George in course of which time have read all the books you mention on the subject of law. ... although I shall most probably be glad some time hence to acquire more by the practice of the law (if I have it in my power) I would still wish to prosecute my studies on the most liberal plan to qualify myself for any business I might chance to engage in. This if not profitable will be agreeable for surely these acquirments qualify a man not only for publick office, but enable him to bear prosperity or adversity in the capricious turns of fortune, with greater magnanimity & fortitude by giving him resources within himself of pleasure & content, which otherwise he would look for in vain from others. *(Monroe to Thomas Jefferson, 1 October 1781)*

To do justice to the ... scientific part of the subject would require a profound knowledge of astronomy and mathematics in the higher branches, to which the Secretary does not pretend. The House will be aware that a knowledge so comprehensive cannot be acquired without much labour in a long course of study, uninterrupted by other duties. These advantages the Secretary has not enjoyed. *(Report as Secretary of State to Congress on the Establishment of a First Meridian, 1 July 1812)*

Soon after I [arrived at the College of William and Mary], a vacation took place, which lasted two months. I had been examined in Latin and Greek and found well qualified to enter the philosophical school. In that I was put to the study of mathematics, Euclid etc., and composing declamation, for which I was altogether unqualified, being only sixteen years of age. I made therefore a ridiculous figure. The vacation taking place, I applied the whole time to close study, so that when the lectures resumed, I had made such good use of my time, that I obtained the approbation and praise of the professors. *(Monroe to James Monroe Jr., 24 December 1813)*

His notoriously bad handwriting

I send you my decision in the case of Major Hall which, if you can read it, you will have copied & carried into immediate effect. *(Monroe to Daniel Parker, adjutant general of the army, 25 April 1818)*

Romance

A young Lady who either is or pretends to be in love is, you know my dear Mrs. Prevost the most unreasonable creature in existence. If she looks a smile or a frown which does not immediately give or deprive you of happiness (at least to appearances) your company soon becomes very insipid. Each feature has its beauty & each attitude the graces or you have no judgment. But if you are so stupidly insensible of her charms as to deprive your tongue & eyes of every expression of admiration & not only to be silent respecting her but devote them to an absent object, she cannot receive an higher insult nor would she if not restrained by politeness refrain from open resentment. *(Monroe to Theodosia Prevost, 8 November 1778)*

But the Indian women I am told are hansome & some of their young girls are tall quiet majestic & susceptible to the influence of all powerful love. For that little villain is not contented with giving pain & torturing the feelings of those who live in the civiliz'd world, of being the cause of routs, tumults, quarells, illblood & sometimes sheding of blood in the courts of Princes & among the Assemblies of Republicks, but he ranges also in the desert & the wilderness & preys upon the heart of many a portly savage. Well, if these Indian women will not fall in love with me I think I shall not with them. I think we are both secure. (Monroe to John F. Mercer, 8 August 1784)

But how are our friends in Annapolis? The Ladies have not a greater admirer of their charms than myself. The only fault I can accuse them of is one similar to that which Yorick brought against the French nation; "They are too fond of solitude." There is however one who joins to the mildest & happiest disposition, that ever bless'd a person of either sex, just & due regard for society & retir'ment so as to qualify her to make happy whomever she smiles on, or if he is not happy in her arms eternal misery shod be his portion. (Monroe to John F. Mercer, 8 August 1784)

Religion

... tis the summit of christian fortitude and heroism to prevail over the views of this transitory life, and turn the mind on the more lasting happiness of that to come. The blessed influence of heaven is, I hope, on you: beware of heresy, danger, ruin, and perpetual misery await it. But while life remains, it is necessary you should have some thing more than mere repentence to amuse your thoughts on. (Monroe to Pierre Duponceau, 11 April 1778)

A proper reverence for our Maker, and indeed religion in general, leaving all men however, free to act agreeable to the dictates of their own consciences, will ever meet my approbation and support. (Monroe to clergy of Portland, Maine, 16 July 1817)

Farms and Farming

For sale, the fifth January next, on the premises, about 500 acres of land in Westmoreland county on Monroe's creek, within a mile and a half of Potomack river. It is perfectly level and rich; has standing on it, a quantity of valuable oak timber, an excellent apple and peach orchard, and where it adjoins the creek, large marshes which with part of the adjoining land, may be turned into a good meadow. There are also, on the tract, a dwelling-house with a passage and several rooms below and above, with a kitchen, barn, stables and other necessary out-houses. The time and means of payment will be ascertained on the day of sale, and made as convenient as possible to the purchaser. *([Richmond] Virginia Gazette, 23 December 1780)*

The truth is that I have become for the first time in my life much engaged & much attached to my farm & to the duties connected with it. I had received from Bordeaux cuttings from vines on all the estates in that quarter, which I had placed in my ground, & which are thriving there. I had it in contemplation to abridge, in a very small compass, Chaptal's work on the culture of the vine, & the making wine, which important service will I fear be lost to the publick by my having left home. You must not however infer any thing unfavorable to my agricultural acquirements. I can assure you that I had made some improvements in the product & appearance of my property in Albemarle. I had sown much clover seed, & covered the ground with plaister of Paris, & derived considerable advantage from the crop of hay last summer & autumn. I had undoubtedly the best clover in the county, & most ground appropriated to it. My industry was a subject of mirth to the old planters & farmers at the commencement but they had ceased to laugh at my experiments before the end of the year. *(Monroe to William Short, 16 February 1811)*

The only hope of placing my affairs on a tolerable footing consists in the increase of my crops, by keeping my farm together, improving my land by a system of manuring it, & selling after a while a portion to save the residence. *(Monroe to Fulwar Skipwith, 27 October 1812)*

For sale, on the premises, on Little river in Loudoun county, Virginia, on the first Monday in August next; a tract of land, of about 2000 acres, 33 miles from [Washington], and likewise from Alexandria. As this land has been heretofore advertised, and particularly described, it is sufficient now to state, that it is of excellent quality, well adapted to the use of the plaister of Paris, well timbered, and watered, Little river passing through the middle of it, a bold & never failing stream; affording a fall of nearly 40 feet within the limits of the tract: that it lies in a populous & healthy country, just below the small village of Aldie, and that the turnpike from the Blue Ridge to Alexandria touches it: that there are several good farm houses on it, with orchards, and a new grist & saw mill, on a stream which empties into Little river. It will be divided into small tracts to suit purchasers. One fourth of the purchase money will be expected, when deeds are made, and a credit of three equal annual instalments given for the balance. At the same time will be sold, about 300 head of Merino Sheep, of the full & mixed blood, upwards of 20 head of horses & mules, with the stock of cattle, hogs, & farming utensils belonging to the estate. *([Washington] National Intelligencer, 28 May 1816)*

Ash Lawn-Highland

I wish every preparation for our final repose, I mean from active life, be on the farm adjoining yours. To this object my attention will be turned whilst abroad and I will endeavor to bring back what will contribute to its comforts. *(Monroe to Thomas Jefferson, 17 June 1794)*

Mr. Jefferson proposes to have a house built for me on my plantation near him, & to which I have agreed under conditions that will make the burden as light as possible upon him. For this purpose I am about to send 2 plans to him submitting both to his judgement & contemplate accepting the offer of a skillful mason here, who wishes to emigrate & settle with us, to execute the work. I wish yourself & Mr. Jones to see the plans & council with Mr. Jefferson upon the subject. *(Monroe to James Madison, 20 January 1796)*

If I can place the funds I shall begin to trouble you about windows etc. as my cabin castle goes on. *(Monroe to Thomas Jefferson, 27 November 1797)*

There wo'd be nothing extraordinary in your coming up to assist me in arrangements there, and bringing Mrs. Madison with you, which I earnestly wish you do next week…. Our house is unfinished in all respects, the yard in confusion, etc. but you shall have a warm chamber and made as comfortable as we can make you. *(Monroe to James Madison, 22 November 1799)*

It has given Mrs. Monroe and myself much concern that our home and establishment in Albemarle, were so limited and in such a state, as to render it impossible for us to make you and your worthy mother and your children comfortable in it. It is a small unfinished cottage affording accommodation insufficient for our small family. It was intended as a temporary one when built, but our absence and other causes prevented our erecting any other since. *(Monroe to Fulwar Skipwith, 12 June 1810)*

3500 acres about 2000 of which are the best mountain quality…. It is five miles from Charlottesville and six from the University. Of its advantageous situation for health and society, no remark need be made there. The estate has all the usual improvements on it, a commodious dwelling house, buildings for servants, and other domestic purposes, good stables, two barns with threshing machine, a grist and sawmill with good houses for managers and laborers, well noted for each purpose, and all in good repair. The tract may be divided advantageously, into several parts, and will be so disposed of if desired… the furniture and stock may be sold with the land. *(Richmond Enquirer, 8 November 1825)*

Retirement

I shall be heartily rejoiced when the term of my service expires, & I may return home in peace with my family, on whom, and especially on Mrs. Monroe, the burdens & cares of my long public service, have borne too heavily. *(Monroe to Thomas Jefferson, 31 October 1824)*

In Albemarle, [where] I expected and wished to have pass'd the remainder of my days, I had laid the foundation with some small professional aid, of independence, which had I remained at home a few years longer, would, I have no doubt, have been completed. By my public employments, and especially those abroad, this hope, has been defeated, and such is actually my situation, that I do not think the grant of my claims will nearly relieve me, by which I mean, will leave me enough to exist in tolerable comfort with my family. *(Monroe to Thomas Jefferson, 13 February 1826)*

It is now three weeks, since I have been confined to my room, & till within a few days, to my bed, by a severe cold & fever. The fever has left me, & in all other respects, the disease has abated, so that I am on the recovery, but I am still weak. This is the second attack, I have had, with the winter, the former proceeding from the fall of my horse, by which I sustained, a severe wound in my leg, which is healed. *(Monroe to unknown, 21 March 1829)*

My pursuits at home are interesting. My mind is not inactive, and in the employment given to it, a review of past occurrences in which I have acted, and of which I have been a witness, occupies a large portion of my time. *(Monroe to Lafayette, 2 May 1829)*

I take exercise on horseback daily, when the weather permits, but I ride a few miles only.... I hope when the weather becomes settled, and I may pursue a regular system of exercizes, that my health will be restored. *(Monroe to Charles Everett, 18 May 1830)*

On great consideration, regarding my weak state of health and advanc'd years, I have thought it adviseable, to comply with the wishes of my family, & remain with them here [in New York City], with such an establishment as I may be able to make, but which I hope will be comfortable. *(Monroe to unknown, 24 March 1831)*

It is painful to me to sell [Oak Hill], from many considerations, among which the separation of me from my friends in the county, has its weight.... But I could accomplish no object, without the sale. It is my intention, if my health will permit, to return to it, sometime next month.... *(Monroe to unknown, 24 March 1831)*

A Selection of Portraits and Views

James Monroe
by Gilbert Stuart (National Gallery of Art)

The pungent anecdotes and witticisms of [Gilbert Stuart], evidently delighted the President; his sober countenance was often distorted, and all the various passions so exposed, that the ingenious Artist has in truth so engrafted them into the image, that the picture is considered to be a most happy one even for Stuart. ([Boston] Columbian Centinel, 30 July 1817)

Quotations of James Monroe

James Monroe
by Samuel F. B. Morse (Charleston (SC) City Hall)

I have been here nearly a fortnight; I commenced the President's portrait on Monday, and shall finish it tomorrow; I have succeeded to my satisfaction, and what is better to the satisfaction of himself & family, so much so that one of his daughters wishes me to copy the head for her; they all say that mine is the best that has been taken to him, the daughter told me, (she said in secret,) that her father was delighted with it and said it was the only one that in his opinion looked like him, and this too with Stuart's in the room. (Samuel F. B. Morse to Jedidiah Morse, 17 December 1820)

Elizabeth Monroe
by Louis Sené (James Monroe Museum)

The night after you left us our friend Monro was married & next morning decamp'd for Long Island with the little smiling Venus in his Arms, where they have taken house, to avoid fulsome Complements during their first Transports & we have not as yet seen him in Town. (Stephen M. Mitchell to William S. Johnson, 21 February 1786)

Elizabeth Monroe
by Raphaelle Peale
(James Monroe Museum)

It is a remark, which it would be unpardonable to withhold, that it was improbable for any female to have fulfilled all the duties of the partner of such cares, and of a wife and parent, with more attention, delicacy and propriety than she has done. (Autobiography of James Monroe)

Elizabeth Monroe
by Frances Maury Burke, after John Vanderlyn
(James Monroe Museum)

With Mrs. Monroe I am really in love. . . . She is charming and very beautiful. She did me the honor of asking to be introduced to me and saying "she regret'd very much she was out when I called" &c and, tho we do not believe all these kinds of things it is gratifying to the vanity to hear them. It would not however have flatter'd me half so much from Mrs. Madison as from her. (Margaret Bayard Smith to Jane Kirkpatrick, 5 December 1816)

Eliza Monroe
by unknown artist
(James Monroe Museum)

Mrs. Monroe hath added a daughter to our society who tho' noisy, contributes greatly to its amusement. (Monroe to Thomas Jefferson, 27 July 1787)

Maria Monroe
by Pietro Cardelli
(James Monroe Museum)

Maria promises to afford us all the gratification, as she grows up, which parents can expect from a fine child. Her education forms the principal occupation of her mother, who takes much delight in it. (Monroe to Francis Baring, 10 August 1809)

Eliza Monroe Hay
by S. Canuson
(Ash Lawn-Highland)

Mrs. Hay, whom you know to be remarkably gay and lively, when a girl, is now a retired, sedate and diligent domestic character, delighted only with her own family and the society of her mother and sister. (Monroe to Fulwar Skipwith, 12 August 1813)

George Hay
by Cephas Thompson
(Ash Lawn-Highland)

Mr Hay is one of the most tender and affectionate husbands, greatly attached to her and she to him. (Elizabeth Trist to Catherine Bache, 10 July 1809)

Maria Monroe Gouverneur
by Charles Bird King
(Ash Lawn-Highland)

MARRIED. On Thursday evening, March 9, in Washington City, by the Rev. Mr. Hawley, Samuel Lawrence Gouverneur, Esq. of New-York to Miss Maria Hester Monroe, youngest daughter of James Monroe, President of the United States. (Hampden Federalist, 22 March 1820)

Samuel Lawrence Gouverneur
(James Monroe Museum)

Samuel Lawrence Gouverneur of New York was this day married to Maria Hester Monroe, The President's youngest daughter. The parties are cousins by the mother's side, and Gouverneur has been nearly these two years in the Presidents family, acting as his private Secretary.... (John Quincy Adams diary, 9 March 1820)

Joseph J. Monroe
attributed to Ezra Ames (James Monroe Museum)

He is now with me reading the law & applies to it with great assiduity. I think his genius equal to any thing he may undertake & I have no doubt of the necessary exertions on his part for the future. (Monroe to Thomas Jefferson, 16 January 1790)

Andrew Monroe
by unknown artist (James Monroe Museum)

He is an honest good hearted man.... (Monroe to James Monroe, Jr., 9 May 1814)

Highland (Ash Lawn-Highland)
I have finally decided to call my place here "Highland." (Monroe to Thomas Jefferson, 9 September 1818)

Highland (Ash Lawn-Highland)
I have made some small changes. The three rooms in which the servants lodged below the well, have been finished inside, painted and made habitable for friends. I have a new house with two rooms framed just below the present one, for lodgers. (Monroe to George Hay, 6 September 1818)

Monroe on Public Affairs

American Revolution

The day on which the American Congress declared the thirteen British Colonies free and independent States was a very important day to mankind. If we critically examine the events of modern times or look back into the records of past ages we shall find nothing like it in the annals of nations. It was important as a measure of policy adopted with a view to secure to the good people of those States the great objects of the controversy. It was important as it dismembered the British empire and erected an independent power in the western hemisphere that was likely soon to be felt in all the great concerns of the eastern. But it was much more important as it introduced a system of government founded on the equal rights and sovereignty of the people under forms more perfect than any that were ever known before. *(Undated)*

When the moment arrived which was to degrade and humiliate the American people to a condition with the slaves of the East, or present to the world the extraordinary spectacle of an independent power in this hemisphere, with the example of a government founded in a great measure on new principles, they proved themselves equal to the crisis. They declared themselves an independent people and by an heroick exertion made themselves so. *(Annual message to the Virginia General Assembly, 7 December 1801)*

The people of America, among whom there was no superior, contended in a common struggle for their equal rights. In that great cause, they sustained with unexampled fortitude, through a long and arduous conflict, every calamity to which savage war is subject, in its worst form. They looked forward to peace, and the happy order of things which would grow out of it, for the reward of their toils, their sufferings and their dangers, and they will not be disappointed. *(Annual message to the Virginia General Assembly, 7 December 1801)*

No approbation can be more dear to me than that of those with whom I have had the honour to share the common toils and perils of the war for our Independence. We were embarked in the same sacred cause of liberty, and we have lived to enjoy the reward of our common labours. Many of our companions in arms fell in the field before our independence was achieved and many, less fortunate than ourselves, lived not to witness the perfect fulfillment of their hopes in the prosperity & happiness of our country. You do but justice to yourselves in claiming the confidence of your country, that you can never desert the standard of freedom. You fought to obtain it in times when men's hearts & principles were severely tried, and your public sacrifices and honorable actions are the best pledges of your sincere and devoted attachment to our excellent constitution. May your children never forget the sacred duties devolved on them to preserve the inheritance so gallantly acquired by their fathers. May they cultivate the same manly patriotism, the same disinterested friendship and the same political integrity, which has distinguished you, and thus unite in perpetuating the social concord and public virtue on which the future prosperity of our country must essentially depend. *(Monroe to the Massachusetts Society of the Cincinnati, 4 July 1817)*

It is impossible to approach Bunker Hill, where the war of the revolution commenced, with so much honor to the nation, without being deeply affected. The blood spilt here roused the whole American people, and united them in a common cause in defence of their rights—That union will never be broken. *(Speech at Charlestown, Massachusetts, 5 July 1817)*

In recurring to the great events which characterize our revolutionary struggle, we see every thing in the conduct of those who guided our councils, and fought our battles, to command our admiration and gratitude. By that great struggle we asserted and achieved our independence; by it was laid the foundation on which our present happy constitution was erected, and our equal rights and liberties completely secured. *(Speech at Georgetown, South Carolina, 22 April 1819)*

Civic Virtue

The constituted authorities and the good people of this Commonwealth [Virginia] are attached to the Union and cherish it with their fondest wishes. The colonization of their Ancestors in this western world was generally from the same Country, at the same time and produced by the same cause: they alike groaned under an oppression which repressed their growth and checked their prosperity: they fought and bled in the same battles in defence of the same rights, and have since experienced with unexampled harmony and unanimity, a variety of interesting occurrences which admonish them they still are and ought to remain forever United. *(Annual message to the General Assembly of Virginia, 1 December 1800)*

May the Citizens of the U. States never forget, that the preservation of American Liberty depends on the preservation of the American Union *(Toast at dinner in Petersburg, VA, 29 January 1801)*

To preserve the sovereignty in the hands of the people it is not necessary, however desireable, that every person should be qualified to fill every office in the State. It is sufficient that the mass of the people possess a correct knowledge of the principles of the government, of their duties and those of their representatives, and that they be attentive to the performance of them. *(Annual message to the Virginia General Assembly, 7 December 1801)*

The measures of improvement which I have thought it my duty to bring to your view especially in the interior navigation of our country, and the publick buildings in this city, are proofs of a policy which is equally respectable for its wisdom and liberality. They exhibit an elevation of mind and a foresight which become the representatives of freemen. They are obviously the offspring of the same spirit which inspired the people of America with the bold design to undertake and the courage to achieve their ever memorable revolution. It is a spirit which ought never to become inactive, but should be cherished, excited and directed to its proper object, the publick good. *(Annual message to the Virginia General Assembly, 7 December 1801)*

It is believed that it is the practice of all government to dedicate certain days to publick festivity. They give relaxation from labor, promote friendly intercourse among the people, and harmonize the society. In the European monarchies it is the practice of the people to celebrate the birthday of their King. Thus they degrade themselves by an unbecoming personal idolatry. With us it is the practice to celebrate the birthday of principle. *(Monroe to Larkin Smith, 28 January 1802)*

The United States are certainly the most enlightened people on earth. We are rapidly advancing in the road to national pre-eminence. Nothing but union is wanting to make us a great people. The present time affords the happiest presages that this union is fast consummating. It cannot be otherwise. I daily see greater proofs of it. The further I advance in my progress through the country, the more I perceive that we are all Americans—that we compose but one family—that our republican institutions will be supported and perpetuated by the united zeal and patriotism of all. Nothing could give me greater satisfaction than to behold a perfect union among ourselves—an union which, as I before observed, is all we can want to make us powerful and respected—an union, also, which is necessary to restore to social intercourse its former charms, and to render our happiness, as a nation, unmixed and complete. *(Speech at Kennebunk, Maine, 15 July 1817)*

In the unexampled prosperity of our country we see all the predictions which had been formed of the excellence of our political institutions completely verified. A people prosperous and happy; a government formed by them, administered exclusively for their advantage; those called to public trusts seeking to merit, by an upright conduct, their approbation, and prizing it above all other rewards. That this state of things may last forever, should be the object of our increasing prayers to the Supreme Ruler of the world. That it will last forever cannot be doubted, provided the people retain the same degree of intelligence and virtue which enabled them to surmount the difficulties to which they were exposed. *(Speech at Georgetown, South Carolina, 22 April 1819)*

The People of the United States—they constitute but one family: may the bond which united them together as brethren and freemen be eternal! *(Toast at dinner in Savannah, GA, 11 May 1819)*

I cannot conclude this communication, the last of the kind which I shall have to make, without recollecting with great sensibility and heartfelt gratitude the many instances of the public confidence and the generous support with which I have been honored. Having commenced my service in early youth, and continued it since with few and short intervals, I have witnessed the great difficulties to which our Union has been exposed, and admired the virtue and intelligence with which they have been surmounted. From the present prosperous and happy state I derive a gratification which I cannot express. That these blessings may be preserved and perpetuated will be the object of my fervent and unceasing prayers to the Supreme Ruler of the Universe. *(Annual message to Congress, 7 December 1824)*

Government

The people of France may conquer their liberties & merit to be free, but without a good government it will be impossible to preserve them. *(Monroe to Thomas Jefferson, 23 June 1795)*

There have been two parties in this country, one whose views are honest, benevolent, republican; the other with views unfriendly to the rights of the people. The latter has enjoyed the govt for 12 years past and greatly abused the trust.... It was on principle that the late change in the administration was made, not by accommodation on the part of the republicans, who sought nothing unreasonable & therefore yielded nothing, but by the honest part of the federalists abandoning their leaders when they saw their confidence was misplac'd & uniting their force to that of the republican party.... The object now is to restore the govt to its principles, amend its defects, reform abuses and introduce order and economy in the administration. *(Monroe to Thomas Jefferson, 18 March 1801)*

In our whole system, national and State, we have shunned all the defects which unceasingly preyed on the vitals and destroyed the ancient Republics. In them there were distinct orders, a nobility and a people, or the people governed in one assembly. Thus, in the one instance there was a perpetual conflict between the orders in society for the ascendency, in which the victory of either terminated in the overthrow of the government and the ruin of the state; in the other, in which the people governed in a body, and whose dominion seldom exceeded the dimension of a county in one of our States, a tumultuous and disorderly movement permitted only a transitory existence. In this great nation there is but one order, that of the people, whose power, by a peculiarly happy improvement of the representative principle, is transferred from them, without impairing in the slightest degree their sovereignty, to bodies of their own creation, and to persons elected by themselves, in the full extent necessary for all the purposes of free, enlightened, and efficient government. *(Second inaugural address, 5 March 1821)*

Whatever shakes our system, or menaces it, will create a despondence throughout the civilized world. They all look to us, and will give up their cause as lost if we shew a doubt of success. *(Annual message to Congress, 2 December 1823)*

The people being with us exclusively the sovereign, it is indispensible that full information be laid before them on all important subjects, to enable them to exercise that high power with complete effect. If kept in the dark, they must be incompetent to it. We are all liable to error, and those who are engaged in the management of public affairs are more subject to excitement and to be led astray by their particular interests and passions than the great body of our constituents, who, living at home in the pursuit of their ordinary avocations, are calm but deeply interested spectators of events and of the conduct of those who are parties to them. To the people every department of the Government and every individual in each are responsible, and the more full their information the better they can judge of the wisdom of the policy pursued and of the conduct of each in regard to it. From their dispassionate judgment much aid may always be obtained, while their approbation will form the greatest incentive and most gratifying reward for virtuous actions, and the dread of their censure the best security against the abuse of their confidence. Their interests in all vital questions are the same, and the bond, by sentiment as well as by interest, will be proportionably strengthened as they are better informed of the real state of public affairs, especially in difficult conjunctures. It is by such knowledge that local prejudices and jealousies are surmounted, and that a national policy, extending its fostering care and protection to all the great interests of our Union, is formed and steadily adhered to. (*Annual message to Congress, 2 December 1823*)

Slavery

I find by your letter... that you think Sierra Leone, on the coast of Africa, a suitable place for the establishment of our insurgent slaves, that it may also become so for those who are or may hereafter be emancipated.... It appears that slavery is prohibited in that settlement, hence it follows that we cannot expect permission to send any who are not free to it. In directing our attention to Africa for an Asylum for insurgents it is strongly implied that the Legislature intended they should be free when landed there, as it is not known that there exists any market on that coast for the purchase of slaves from other countries.... I do not know that such an arrangement would be practicable in any country, but it would certainly be a very fortunate attainment if we could make these people instrumental in their own emancipation, by a process gradual and certain, on principles consistent with humanity, without expense or inconvenience to ourselves. (*Monroe to Thomas Jefferson, 11 June 1802*)

I had the pleasure to receive your favor of the 10th two days since, and your essay on the abolition of the slave trade, this afternoon. I anticipate much satisfaction in the perusal of this work, which is indeed on a very interesting subject. I congratulate you sincerely on the progress which is made in that business, which promises to be attended with complete success in [Great Britain] & in the U States of America. It is a very honorable trait in the character of both countries to have combined their efforts for the accomplishment of so benevolent and humane an object. It does them more credit than the combinations which usually take place among nations, which are for the destruction not the preservation of the human race. *(Monroe to William Wilberforce, 13 February 1807)*

The God who made us made the black people, & they ought not to be treated with barbarity. *(Monroe to Charles Everett, 23 March 1812)*

They have been raised by our own Citizens, who take an interest in their welfare not as property only, but as persons. Much interest and sympathy are felt by the parties for each other. Their condition is, in general, as favorable as that of the peasantry in Europe, and much better than it is in some Countries. This I know to be the sentiment of Mr. Wilberforce, who has long taken the lead in the abolition of the slave trade. When in England I gave him a sketch of the treatment of slaves in the United States generally, and such was his remarks on seeing it. *(Monroe to Thomas Pinckney, 6 April 1815)*

The object of this institution is to promote the colonizing of the free people of color in the United States, with their own consent, in Africa, or wherever else the wisdom of the General Government may recommend.... [Blacks] can never here enjoy all the advantages, social and political, of freemen. If the Constitution and the laws were even to proclaim them entitled to these advantages, such is the force of habit and of prejudice, that the constitution and the laws, would in this respect be altogether inoperative. *(Monroe to unknown, 22 September 1817)*

Due attention has likewise been paid to the suppression of the slave trade, in compliance with a law of the last session. Orders have been given to the commanders of all our public ships to seize all vessels navigated under our flag engaged in that trade, and to bring them in to be proceeded against in the manner prescribed by that law. It is hoped that these vigorous measures, supported by like acts by other nations, will soon terminate a commerce so disgraceful to the civilized world. *(Annual message to Congress, 7 December 1819)*

In compliance with a Resolution of the House of Representatives adopted at their last session, instructions have been given to all the ministers of the United States to propose the proscription of the African slave trade by classing it under the denomination of piracy. Should this proposal be acceded to, it is not doubted that this odious and criminal practice will be promptly and entirely suppressed. *(Annual message to Congress, 2 December 1823)*

I have always been friendly to an emancipation, & transportation from the country, with a view, to make an experiment, of the practicability of the scheme. I have wished also to let it be seen by our fellow citizens in those states, where there are no slaves, that we to the south, are as friendly to liberty, as they are, and that the existence of slavery among us, is one of the evils still remaining, incident to our Colonial system, and of which, to so great a height had it risen, that we have not yet been able to rid ourselves. *(Monroe to John Mason, 31 August 1829)*

Education

May we not hope as the country becomes exonerated from debt, publick & private, some considerable advance may be made for the establishment of [a state university]? *(Monroe to Thomas Jefferson, 17 July 1792)*

These young men are penetrated with a great desire to see the college [William & Mary], wh rear'd the youth who had firmness and virtue sufficient to stem the current which threatened our liberties. If I were ever to compose an oration, and deliver it at a publick festival, it wod be in favor of our alma mater and the noble effort her offspring has lately made in defense of the holy cause of mankind. *(Monroe to St. George Tucker, 18 November 1798)*

In a government founded on the sovereignty of the people the education of youth is an object of the first importance. In such a government knowledge should be diffused throughout the whole society, and for that purpose the means of acquiring it made not only practicable but easy to every citizen.... It is only when the people become ignorant and corrupt that their representatives forget their duty and aspire to the sovereignty. In such a government education should not be left to the care of the individuals only. Being a high publick concern, it ought to be provided for by the government itself.... It is believed that no measure which can be adopted would contribute more to the security of free government, or to the harmony of its movements, than a well planned system of instruction.... At present a considerable sum is expended annually by the citizens of every county in the education of youth. The poorest citizen contributes something to the instruction of his offspring. There is scarce an inhabitant of our country so lost to the claims of nature and to every just and generous sentiment as to abandon his children to brutal ignorance. The wealthy contribute large sums to that object, since they are compelled generally to entertain tutors at home or send their children to be educated at a distance, in either case at great expense. It cannot be doubted if the sum which is now expended in every county in the education of youth, was collected into one fund and committed to the care of discreet agents, they would be able to procure excellent instructors, and establish seminaries in every neighbourhood.... It is certain that by the establishment of such a number of seminaries in the several counties, under the care of skilful preceptors, knowledge would be more generally diffused, and the morality of the children, who would be instructed in the presence of the parents, better preserved. It is equally certain that such system of instruction would give support to the principle of the government itself. It would draw the youth of the country into society together by means whereof they would become acquainted and form friendships which would remain through life; friendships which would equally promote the social harmony of the State, and the comfort and happiness of the individuals who compose it. (*Annual message to the Virginia General Assembly, 7 December 1801*)

An institution which endeavors to rear American youth in the pure love of truth and duty, and while it enlightens their minds by ingenious and liberal studies, endeavors to awaken a love of country, to soften local prejudices and to inculcate Christian faith and charity, cannot but acquire, as it deserves, the confidence of the wise and good.... I shall always take a lively interest in its prosperity. *(Monroe to John Kirkland, president of Harvard University, 12 July 1817)*

I take a deep interest as a parent and a citizen, in the success of female education; and have been delighted, wherever I have been, to witness the attention paid to it. *(Remarks at Windsor Female Academy, Windsor, Vermont, 22 July 1817)*

In providing for the prosperity and happiness of a country, a careful attention to literary institutions, and the education of youth ought ever to occupy a high place. To the youth we must look with an eye of deep interest—they are the hope of our country—and I cannot omit mentioning, the peculiar gratification I have received from observing the growth of literary institutions, & the attention which is paid to the instruction of youth, and which is certainly the best & most permanent basis, on which our privileges, civil and religious, can be founded. *(Speech at Washington College, Washington, Pennsylvania, 4 September 1817)*

I cannot express in terms too strong, the satisfaction which I derive from a view of this Seminary, established by private munificence, for the education of the female sex, having already under its charge 200 females, and exhibiting by its system of instruction, and management, so fair a prospect of advantage to the country. The female presents capacities for improvement, and has equal claims to it, with the other sex. Without intermitting our attention to the improvement of the one, let us extend it alike to the other. Its beneficial effect will be felt on all the high interests of the community. *(Speech at the Nashville Female Academy, Nashville, Tennessee, 10 June 1819)*

A military instructor [at the University of Virginia] whose duty it should be, to call the roll, and parade the youth, at such times as should be appointed, to instruct them in military tactics and see that they are in place. To educate the youth in all the sciences, and rear them to elevated and useful purposes, an appeal must be made to generous and noble sentiments, but at the same time the discipline must be exact and strict. Their duties should be regulated by the hour, and they should always be in place at the time appointed. A departure from the rule is sure to degenerate into licentiousness. *(Monroe to Sylvanus Thayer, 25 August 1828)*

Defense

The militia law is ... a subject which it is thought merits the attention of the Legislature. It is one of great importance as the militia of a free state is justly considered the bulwark of its liberty. No people are secure in the enjoyment of their rights who keep within their limits a strong military force, trained to subordination and accustomed to obey with reverence the orders of its chief.... [F]ree men should not rely on others for the protection of an interest for which they are personally responsible, and from which they have no right to shrink. *(Annual message to the Virginia General Assembly, 7 December 1801)*

I am persuaded that a systematic plan of fortifying our seaports ought to be adopted; that it would be grateful to our citizens interested cannot be doubted; that it would produce an useful effect abroad is certain. *(Monroe to Thomas Jefferson, 18 May 1803)*

To secure us against these dangers our coast and inland frontiers should be fortified, our Army and Navy regulated upon just principles as to the force of each, be kept in perfect order, and our militia placed on the best practicable footing.... Our land and naval forces should be moderate, but adequate to the necessary purposes.... *(First inaugural address, 4 March 1817)*

It is my intention to take a view of the fortifications & other public works, along our coast, and on our Inland frontier, in the course of this approaching summer. I think that such a trip, devoted strictly to its object, will be useful, as well by drawing the public attention to such works, as by enabling me to perform the duties assigned to me, in regard to them, with greater advantage. *(Monroe to William Jones, 22 April 1817)*

It is only by making adequate preparation for war, now that we are blessed with peace that we can hope to avert that calamity in future. It is only by a vigorous prosecution of the war, when it becomes inevitable, that its evils can be mitigated, and an honorable peace be soon restored. *(Speech at New London, Connecticut, 25 June 1817)*

Indians

My Red Children: You cannot become civilized 'till you advance one step farther. You know that, among my white children, each one has his own land separate from all others. You ought to do the same. You ought to divide your lands among families, into lots sufficiently large to maintain a family according to its size.... By thus dividing your land, each one could then say, this is mine, and he would have inducements to put up good houses on it and improve his land by cultivation. *(Monroe to the Seneca, 15 January 1819)*

I am much pleased with the progress made in instructing the Indian youth, & have no doubt that in this mode, that is, by acting on the youthful mind, the [Cherokee] nation, & other nations, may be civilized. It merits therefore all the encouragement that the Government can give it. *(Monroe to R. J. Meigs, 27 May 1819)*

I have no hesitation, however, to declare it as my opinion that the Indian title was not affected in the slightest circumstance by the compact with Georgia, and that there is no obligation on the United States to remove the Indians by force. The express stipulation of the compact that their title should be extinguished at the expense of the United States when it may be done peaceably and on reasonable conditions is a full proof that it was the clear and distinct understanding of both parties to it that the Indians had a right to the territory, in the disposal of which they were to be regarded as free agents. An attempt to remove them by force would, in my opinion, be unjust. In the future measures to be adopted in regard to the Indians within our limits, and, in consequence, within the limits of any State, the United States have duties to perform and a character to sustain to which they ought not to be indifferent. At an early period their improvement in the arts of civilized life was made an object with the Government, and that has since been persevered in. This policy was dictated by motives of humanity to the aborigines of the country, and under a firm conviction that the right to adopt and pursue it was equally applicable to all the tribes within our limits. (*Message to Congress, 30 March 1824*)

Experience has shown that unless the tribes be civilized they can never be incorporated into our system in any form whatever. It has likewise shown that in the regular augmentation of our population with the extension of our settlements their situation will become deplorable, if their extinction is not menaced. Some well-digested plan which will rescue them from such calamities is due to their rights, to the rights of humanity, and to the honor of the nation. Their civilization is indispensible to their safety, and this can be accomplished only by degrees. The process must begin with the infant state, through whom some effect may be wrought on the parental. Difficulties of the most serious character present themselves to the attainment of this very desirable result on the territory on which they now reside. To remove them from it by force, even with a view to their own security and happiness, would be revolting to humanity and utterly unjustifiable. Between the limits of our present States and Territories and the Rocky Mountains and Mexico there is a vast territory to which they might be invited with inducements which might be successful. It is thought if that territory should be divided into districts by previous agreement with the tribes now residing there and civil governments be established in each, with schools for every branch of instruction in literature and the arts of civilized life, that all the tribes now within our limits might gradually be drawn there. The execution of this plan would necessarily be attended with expense, and that not inconsiderable, but it is doubted whether any other can be devised which would be less liable to that objection or more likely to succeed. *(Annual address to Congress, 7 December 1824)*

The Presidency

I should be destitute of feeling if I was not deeply affected by the strong proof which my fellow-citizens have given me of their confidence in calling me to the high office whose functions I am about to assume. As the expression of their good opinion of my conduct in the public service, I derive from it a gratification which those who are conscious of having done all that they could to merit it can alone feel. My sensibility is increased by a just estimate of the importance of the trust and of the nature and extent of its duties, with the proper discharge of which the highest interests of a great and free people are intimately connected. Conscious of my own deficiency, I can not enter on these duties without great anxiety for the result. From a just responsibility I will never shrink, calculating with confidence that in my best efforts to promote the public welfare my motives will always be duly appreciated and my conduct viewed with that candor and indulgence which I have experienced in other stations. *(First inaugural address, 4 March 1817)*

Devoted to the principles of our government from my earliest youth, and satisfied that the great blessings which we enjoy are, under Divine Providence, imputable to that great cause, it will be the object of my constant and zealous efforts, to give to those principles their best effect—Should I, by these efforts contribute, in any degree, to the happiness of my fellow-citizens, I shall derive from it the highest gratification of which my mind is susceptible. *(Speech at New York City, 11 June 1817)*

It is to the execution of these [defensive] works, both land and naval, and under a thorough conviction that by hastening their completion I should render the best service to my country and give the most effectual support to our free republican system of government that my humble faculties would admit of, that I have devoted so much of my time and labor to this great system of national policy since I came into this office and shall continue to do it until my retirement from it at the end of your next session. (*Monroe to the House of Representatives, 30 January 1824*)

The Federalists

... a gang of greater scoundrels never lived. We are to dance on their birth night, forsooth, and say they are great and good men, when we know they are little people. I think the spirit of that idle propensity is dying away & that the good sense of the people is breaking thro' the prejudice which has long chained them down. (*Monroe to Thomas Jefferson, 26 March 1798*)

Louisiana

The purchase of the whole of Louisiana, tho' not contemplated is nevertheless a measure founded on the principles and justified by the policy of our instructions, provided it be thought a good bargain. The only difference between the acquisition we have made, and that which we were instructed to make in that respect, is, that a favorable occasion presenting itself which indeed was not anticipated by the administration, in the measure which led to that event and laid the foundation for it, we have gone further than we were instructed to do. (*Monroe to James Madison, 18 May 1803*)

It is equally presumable that England even in case of war would not interfere with our pursuit, much less break with us for obtaining the Floridas. The exclusion of her manufactures from the Continent of Europe, is a principle cause of her present unquiet and distressed situation. It is her interest to cherish the U. States and Russia, as her best markets; a policy which I believe she understands and pursues with sincerity. To be involved in a war with us at this epoch would prove a great calamity to her. I have no doubt that at this time she is neither indifferent respecting our acquisition of Louisiana, and that which we propose to make of the Floridas, or in no situation to oppose it. Indeed it is not improbable that she may wish it, as it weakens these powers, in that quarter and promises to open new markets to her manufactures. *(Monroe to James Madison, 18 May 1803)*

To have contributed in any degree to carry into effect those measures, and justify the wisdom and benevolence of the policy which dictated them, if the result is approved, will always be a source of much delight to me. *(Monroe to Thomas Jefferson, 18 May 1803)*

We have as you will find concluded a treaty & two conventions with [France] for the cession of the whole of Louisiana. I flatter myself that the terms will be thought reasonable when compared with the immense advantages resulting from the acquisition.... I consider this transaction as resulting from the wise & firm tho' moderate measures of the Executive and Congress.... *(Monroe to Senators Mason, Nicholas and Breckinridge, 18 May 1803)*

Reports continue to circulate that the Spanish Government has ceded to Great-Britain the Floridas and Louisiana.... If the British government has accepted a cession of this territory from Spain and is taking measures for its occupancy her conduct must be considered as decidedly hostile to the United States.... *(Monroe to John Quincy Adams, 10 December 1815)*

Great Britain

Shortly afterward, in conversing with Lord Castlereagh & some other gentleman on the rapid growth of the U States, I observed that I was astonished to find persons of distinction by their offices and talents so extremely uninformed on that subject, as they were generally in this country: that in truth they knew as little of us as they did of the cape of good hope. *(Monroe to Thomas Jefferson, 15 March 1804)*

War of 1812

I most sincerely wish that the President could dispose of me, at this juncture, to the military line. If circumstances would permit, and it should be thought that I could render any service, I would in a very few days, join our forces assembling beyond the Ohio, & endeavor to recover the ground we have lost. *(Monroe to Henry Clay, 28 August 1812)*

From the northern army we have nothing which inspires a confident hope, of any brilliant success. The disaffection in that quarter has paralised every effort of the govt & render'd inoperative every law of Congress; I speak comparatively with what might have been expected. On the public mind however a salutary effect is produced even there, by the events which have occurr'd. Misfortune & success, have alike diminished the influence of foreign attachments, & party animosities, and contributed to draw the people closer together. The surrender of our army excited a general grief, and the naval victory a great joy. Inveterate toryism itself was compelled in both instances, to disguise its character & hide its feelings, by appearing to simpathise with those of the nation. If G Britain does not come forward soon and propose honourable conditions, I am convinced that the war will become a national one, & will terminate in the expulsion of her force & power, from the continent. *(Monroe to Henry Clay, 17 September 1812)*

I shall call your attention to the most important grounds of the controversy with Great Britain.... On impressments, as to the right of the United States to be exempted from it, I have nothing new to add.... This degrading practice must cease; our flag must protect the crew; or the United States, cannot consider themselves an independent Nation.... Blockade is the subject, next in point of importance.... [A] principle object in making peace, is to prevent, by the justice and reciprocity of the conditions, a recurrence again to war, for the same cause. If the British Government sincerely wishes to make a durable peace with the United States, it can have no reasonable objection to a just definition of a blockade.... Experience has shewn that Great Britain cannot participate in the dominion and Navigation of the Lakes, without incurring the danger of an early renewal of the War. It was by means of the Lakes that the British Government interfered with, and gained an ascendancy over the Indians, even within our own limits. The effect produced the massacre of our own Citizens, after they were made prisoners, and of defenceless women and children along our frontiers, need not be described.... This alone will prove a fruitful source of controversy; but there are others.... (Monroe to the American peace commissioners, 28 January 1814)

The events of that war are too recent and too deeply impressed on the memory of all to require a development from me. Our commerce had been in a great measure driven from the sea; our Atlantic and inland frontiers were invaded in almost every part; the waste of life along our coast and on some parts of our inland frontiers, to the defense of which our gallant and patriotic citizens were called, was immense, in addition to which not less than $120,000,000 were added at its end to the public debt. (Second inaugural address, 5 March 1821)

Missouri Compromise

I have never known a question so menacing to the tranquility and even the continuance of our Union as the present one.... As however there is a vast portion of intelligence & virtue in the body of the people, & the bond of Union has heretofore prov'd sufficiently strong to triumph over all attempts against it, I have great confidence that this effort will not be less unavailing. (Monroe to Thomas Jefferson, 19 February 1820)

Greece

The mention of Greece fills the mind with the most exalted sentiments and arouses in our bosoms the best feelings of which our nature is susceptible. Superior skill and refinement in the arts, heroic gallantry in action, disinterested patriotism, enthusiastic zeal and devotion in favor of public and personal liberty are associated with our recollections of ancient Greece. That such a country should have been overwhelmed and so long hidden, as it were, from the world under a gloomy despotism has been a cause of unceasing and deep regret to generous minds for ages past. It was natural, therefore, that the reappearance of those people in their original character, contending in favor of their liberties, should produce that great excitement and sympathy in their favor which have been so signally displayed throughout the United States. A strong hope is entertained that these people will recover their independence and resume their equal station among the nations of the earth. *(Annual message to Congress, 3 December 1822)*

Spanish American Independence

It is understood that the colonies in South America have had great success during the present year in the struggle for their independence.... It has long been manifest that it would be impossible for Spain to reduce these colonies by force, and equally so that no condition short of their independence would be satisfactory to them. It may therefore be presumed, and it is earnestly hoped, that the Government of Spain, guided by enlightened and liberal councils, will find it to comport with its interests and due to its magnanimity to terminate this exhausting controversy on that basis. *(Annual message to Congress, 3 December 1821)*

The Provinces belonging to this hemisphere are our neighbors, and have successively, as each portion of the country acquired its independence, pressed their recognition by an appeal to the facts not to be contested, and which they thought gave them a just title to it.... It was incumbent on this Government to look to every important fact and circumstance on which a sound opinion could be formed, which has been done. When we regard, then, the great length of time which this war has been prosecuted, the complete success which has attended it in favor of the Provinces, the present condition of the parties, and the utter inability of Spain to produce any change in it, we are compelled to conclude that its fate is settled, and that the Provinces which have declared their independence and are in the enjoyment of it ought to be recognized. *(Monroe to Congress, 8 March 1822)*

The Monroe Doctrine

In the discussions to which this interest has given rise... the occasion has been judged proper for asserting, as a principle in which the rights and interests of the United States are involved, that the American continents, by the free and independent condition which they have assumed and maintain, are henceforth not to be considered as the subjects for future colonization by any European powers. *(Annual message to Congress, 2 December 1823)*

We owe, therefore, to candor and to the amicable relations existing between the United States and those powers to declare that we should consider any attempt on their part to extend their system to any portion of this hemisphere as dangerous to our peace and safety. With the existing colonies and dependencies of any European power we have not interfered and shall not interfere. But with those Governments who have declared their independence and maintained it, and whose independence we have, on great consideration and on just principles acknowledged, we could not view any interposition for the purpose of oppressing them, or controlling in any other manner their destiny, by any European power in any other light than as the manifestation of an unfriendly disposition toward the United States. *(Annual message to Congress, 2 December 1823)*

Our policy in regard to Europe, which was adopted at an early stage of the wars which have so long agitated that quarter of the globe, nevertheless remain the same, which is, not to interfere in the internal concerns of any of its powers; to consider the government de facto as the legitimate government for us; to cultivate friendly relations with it, and to preserve those relations by a frank, firm, and manly policy, meeting in all instances the just claims of every power, submitting to injuries from none. *(Annual message to Congress, 2 December 1823)*

On the Monroes

James Monroe

Monroe is just setting out from Head Quarters and proposes to go in quest of adventures to the Southward. He seems to be as much of a knight errant as your worship, but as he is an honest fellow, I shall be glad he may find some employment, that will enable him to get knocked in the head in an honorable way. He will relish your black scheme [for raising a battalion of black soldiers] if any thing handsome can be done for him in that line. You know him to be a man of honor a sensible man and a soldier. This makes it unnecessary to me to say anything to interest your friendship for him. You love your country too and he has zeal and capacity to serve it. (*Alexander Hamilton to John Laurens, 22 May 1779*)

I have always asserted that you would appear one of the first characters of this country, if your shyness did not prevent the display of the knowledge and talents you possess. Mr. White tells me you have got rid of this mauvaise honte and only retain a certain degree of recommendatory modesty. (*Charles Lee to Monroe, 18 July 1780*)

Poor Col. Monro! The man is in despair he has written a letter to Gen. Gates telling him that he lost his heart on board the Albany sloop, and fills the sheet with a panygeric upon his fair one. I fear his love did not meet with a return, but we were blind & not acquainted with one half his perfections of person or mind. They were summed up to me this day and amounted to eight which includes every thing that a female can wish or a man envy. He is a member of Congress, rich, young, sensible, well read, lively, and handsome. I forget the other accomplishment, and will not subscribe to the last unless you prove the dimple in his chin to be what constitutes beauty, & I have a doubt about the sixth unless it is agreed that affording subject for gaity & liveliness to the company you are in, is the same thing as being gay & lively yourself. If you are the goddess at whose shrine he worships, inform me of it, that I may think higher of his perfection; his being your choice will have great influence upon me, and stop me often when I might be saucily inclined, for at present he is more the object of my divertion than admiration. *(Sarah Vaughan to Catherine Livingston, 10 October 1784)*

What measures have you taken for establishing yourself near Monticello? Nothing in this world will keep me long from that spot of ultimate repose for me. I keep my eye on yourself and Short for society and do not despair of Madison. *(Thomas Jefferson to Monroe, 11 May 1785)*

In the Opportunity I have had of being with him, I have found him very sensible and agreeable, and possessing those pleasing Manners, which take off from the formality of a new Acquaintance and smooth the Way to Friendship. *(William Temple Franklin to Thomas Jefferson, 18 January 1786)*

I wish to heaven you may continue in the disposition to fix [your residence] in Albemarle. Short will establish himself there, & perhaps Madison may be tempted to do so. This will be society enough, & it will be the sweetener of our lives. Without society, and a society to our taste, humans are never contented. *(Thomas Jefferson to Monroe, 18 December 1786)*

Turn his soul wrong side outwards and there is not a speck on it. *(Thomas Jefferson to James Madison, 30 January 1787)*

All the members of the board are pleasant men to do business with, except Wood, whom you will find crusty & very disagreeable. He however writes well & folds a letter hansomely, in neither of which do you excell. *(John Dawson to Monroe, 19 January 1800)*

It would give us sincere pleasure to see you here, assisting in measures upon which the prosperity of this college [William &

Mary] may soon greatly depend. A meeting of the visitors will be held on Tuesday next. Nothing but the apprehension of exposing you to so long a ride could prevent an official notification of this meeting. If however, you could make it convenient to attend, I know it would be grateful to the College. I am persuaded your presence would be productive of real effect. *(Bishop James Madison to Monroe, 17 March 1802)*

Mr. Madison's friendship and mine to you being so well known the public will have eagle eyes to watch if we grant you any indulgences out of the general rule.... The allowance therefore will be... as proscribed by law. *(Thomas Jefferson to Monroe, 13 January 1803)*

The [Governor] of this Commonwealth is the same [man] who was, not many years ago, the [minister] at Paris. His present office is sufficient evidence of the estimation in which he is held by his native state. In his stature, he is about the middle height of men, rather firmly set, with nothing further remarkable in his person, except his muscular compactness and apparent ability to endure labour. His countenance, when grave, has rather the expression of sternness and irrasibility; a smile, however, (and a smile is not unusual with him in a social circle,) lights it up to a very high advantage, and gives it a most impressive and engaging air of suavity and benevolence. Judging merely from his countenance, he is between the ages of forty-five and fifty years. His dress and personal appearance are those of a plain and modest gentleman. He is a man of soft, polite and even assiduous attentions; but these, although they are always well-timed, judicious and evidently the offspring of an obliging and philanthropic temper, are never performed with the striking and captivating graces of a Marlborough or a Bolingbroke. To be plain, there is often in his manner an inartificial and even an awkward simplicity, which while it provokes the smile of a more polished person, force him to the opinion that Mr. [Monroe] is a man of a most sincere and artless soul.

Nature has given him a mind neither rapid nor rich, and therefore he cannot shine on a subject which is entirely new to him. But to compensate him for this he is endued with a spirit of restless emulation, a judgment strong and clear, and a habit of application which no difficulties can shake, no labours can tire.

With these aids simply, he has qualified himself for the first honours of this country; and a most happy illustration of the truth of the maxim, Quisque, suae fortunae, faber. For his emulation has urged him to perpetual and unremitting inquiry; his patient and unwearied industry has concentrated before him all the lights which others have thrown on the subjects of his consideration, together with all those which his own mind, by repeated efforts, is enabled to strike; while his sober, steady and faithful judgment has saved him from the common error of more quick and brilliant geniuses; the too hasty adoption of specious, but false conclusions.

These qualities render him a safe and an able counsellor. And by their constant exertion, he has amassed a store of knowledge, which, having passed seven times through the crucible, is almost as highly corrected as human knowledge can be; and which certainly may be much more safely relied on than the spontaneous and luxuriant growth of a more fertile, but less chastened mind—"a wild, where weeds and flowers promiscuous shoot."

Having engaged very early, first in the life of a soldier, then of a statesman, then of a laborious practitioner of the law, and finally, again of a politician, his intellectual operations have been almost entirely confined to juridicial and political topics. Indeed, it is easy to perceive, that the mind of a man, engaged in so active a life must possess more native suppleness, versatility and vigour, than that of Mr. [Monroe], to be able to make an advantageous tour of the sciences in the rare interval of importune duties. It is possible that the early habit of contemplating subjects has expanded as the earth itself, with all the relative interests of the great nations thereof, may have inspired him with an indifference, perhaps an inaptitude, for mere point of literature. Algernon Sidney has said that he deems all studies unworthy the serious regard of man, except the study of the principles of just government; and Mr. [Monroe], perhaps, concurs with our countryman in this as well as in his other principles. Whatever may have been the occasion, his acquaintance with the fine arts is certainly very limited and superficial; but, making allowances for his bias towards republicanism, he is a profound and even an eloquent statesmen.

Knowing him to be attached to that political party, who, by their opponents, are called sometimes democrats, sometimes Jacobins; and aware also, that he was a man of warm and even ardent temper, I dreaded much, when I first entered his company, that I should have been shocked and disgusted with the narrow virulent and rancorous invectives of party animosity. How agreeably, how delightfully, was I disappointed! Not one sentiment of intolerance polluted his lips. On the contrary, whether they be the offspring of rational induction, of the habit of surveying men and things on a great scale, of native magnanimity, or of a combination of all those causes, his principles, as far as they were exhibited to me, were forebearing, liberal, widely extended and great.

As the elevated ground, which he already holds, has been gained merely by the dint of application; as every new step which he mounts becomes a mean of increasing his powers still further, by opening a wider horizon to his view, and thus stimulating his enterprise afresh, reinvigorating his habits, multiplying the materials and extending the range of his knowledge; it would be matter of no surprise to me, if, before his death, the world should see him at the head of the American administration. So much for the [governor] of the commonwealth of Virginia: a living, an honourable, an illustrious monument of self-created eminence, worth and greatness! *(William Wirt, The Letters of a British Spy, 1803)*

Today there were no Ladies at Table. My seat at Dinner was between Mr. Jefferson and Mr. Monroe. Placed between the President and the Envoy, I was highly gratified. For besides the Repast of food and drink, which were of the customary good quality, I found both these distinguished Gentlemen very affable and communicative. Mr. M. is to go for New York in a few days, on his way to France. He will proceed thence to Havre de Grace on his Mission. He told me that Mrs. Monroe would accompany him. He appears to have fine conjugal feelings and thought it too hard to cross the Ocean without his amiable consort. Accordingly he takes her with him. *(Samuel L. Mitchill to Catherine Mitchell, 9 February 1803)*

For on the event of this mission [to France] depends the future destinies of this republic ... I am sensible after the measures you have taken for getting into a different line of business, that it will be a great sacrifice on your part and presents from the seasons & other circumstances serious difficulties. But some men were born for the public. Nature by fitting them for the service of the human race on a broad scale, has stamped them with the evidence of their destination & their duty. *(Thomas Jefferson to Monroe, 13 January 1803)*

Mr. Monroe, is I believe honest—a man of plain common sense—practical—but not scientific. *(William Plumer, Memorandum, 16 March 1806)*

Whilst you have been labouring in European Courts to secure and preserve to us, the advantages of peace, and to avert the callamities of war, we have been enjoying the fruits of your labor.... *(Hugh Nelson to Monroe, 21 December 1807)*

Mr. Jefferson is unquestionably your fast friend, and earnestly desirous of advancing your prosperity. The offer of the Orleans Government is proof of that. *(John Taylor to Monroe, 22 February 1808)*

If I should gain any credit, I intend to announce you as the apostle of the plough, and in a late trip near your estate, I found that your having actually worked could be proved. Politicians who know what work is, are what we ploughmen want. *(John Taylor to Monroe, 27 July 1811)*

You will go on fretting yourself and Mrs. Monroe in public stations 'till you have passed the prime of your life; and then retire disgusted and dissatisfied. *(Pierce Butler to Monroe, 22 December 1811)*

Mr. Monroe had gone out for the time being when I arrived at his residence yesterday. He came back shortly afterwards, and I found in him a man of urbanity, who spoke French very well. From the very first one perceives that he has lived in the most distinguished circles; but it is still more pleasing to recognize in him qualities of kindness and good will. *(Baron de Montlezun, 21 September 1816)*

No one can become acquainted with President Monroe, without being enamoured of his simplicity; warmed by his engaging deportment; and charmed by his unaffected conversation. *([New Brunswick, NJ] Fredonian, 12 June 1817)*

The dress of the President has been deservedly noticed in other papers for its neatness and republican simplicity. He wore a plain blue coat, a buff under dress, and a hat and cockade of the revolutionary fashion. It comported with his rank, was adapted to the occasion, and well calculated to excite in the minds of the people, the remembrance of the day which "tried men's souls." *([New Haven] Connecticut Herald, 29 June 1817)*

Mr. James Munroe, the present President of the United States is a large and tall man of dark Complexion & blue eyes & a very grave contenance—and in no wise [foppish] but plane. The day he passed through this place he rode on a gray horse, a plane saddle and a bridle not extraordinary—His dress was blue Broadcloth coat & pantaloons, a light coloured waist coat and a common beaver Hat &c. *(Guerdon Gates Journal, 4 September 1817)*

When President Munroe was on his Tour surrounded by the military, encompassed by citizens, harased by invitations to parties, and applications innumerable for office—some gentleman asked him if he was not compleatly worn out—to which he replied—o no—a little flattery will support a man through great fatigue. . . . *(Abigail Adams to Francis Vanderkemp, 24 July 1818)*

We cannot close this article without mentioning the favorable impression which has been made on all who have seen him by the manners of the President—unostentatious, mild and affable, he unites in his deportment the frank simplicity of a Republican citizen with the dignity which becomes the Chief of a great nation. His manners are as well fitted to win affection as his talents to command respect. *(Edenton [NC] Gazette, 13 April 1819)*

He looked at the buildings & farm, visited the school, & asked questions in the most unaffected & familiar manner: & was pleased to express his approbation of the plan of instruction; particularly as the children were taken into the family, taught to work &c. He thought this the best, & perhaps the only way to civilise & christianise the indians: and assured us he was well pleased with the conduct & improvement of the children.

We had put up, & were finishing a log cabbin for the use of the girls. He said such buildings were not good enough, & advise that we put another kind of building in place of this; that we make it a good two-story house, with brick or stone chimneys, glass windows, &c, & that it be done at the public expence. He also observed, that after this was done, it might perhaps be thought best to build another of the same description for the boys; but we would do this first. *(Journal of the Brainerd, Tennessee, Indian Mission, 27 May 1819)*

I feel with great sensibility the kind expressions of your friendship to me and reciprocate them with warmth and sincerity. If there be a balm for the human soul it is in the affections of others. Ours has stood the test of youth and of age and I feel with fervor that your fame and fortune interests me as strongly as my own. With the wish of every blessing to you I remain ever and affectionately yours. *(Thomas Jefferson to Monroe, 27 September 1821)*

I saw today Mr. Madison & Monroe. The former is a small but very venerable looking old gentleman. The latter would have looked more like a man in his prime. But his buckskin breeches over boots and a long black coat that touched his boot tops cloathed a figure which would have become the days of the 17th century and consequently had not the paternal appearance of his aged colleague. *(Robert Blow to George Blow, 3 October 1826)*

Mr. Monroe has an invaluable library to which I have free access. *(Egbert Watson to Daniel Railey, 1 August 1828)*

There have been few more zealous, indefatigable or useful servants of the public than James Monroe. He was early in life an officer in the Revolutionary war. He has since successively occupied almost every station of public confidence which his native state or the national government could confer. He has maintained his own dignity and that of his country throughout his whole political life and preserved the moderation of his temper amidst all the bickerings of party rancour. His abandoning the course of his education at college for the pursuits of war, his incipient employment in business since have scarcely allowed him leisure for those literary attainments which distinguish Mr. Jefferson and Madison. It would therefore be unfair to expect of him equal qualifications in letters. The duties of his life have called only for a sound judgment and decision of action. *(Francis Walker Gilmer, Sketches of American Statesmen)*

The character of Mr. M's mind is formed for business and action rather than for fine intellectual exertion. In his intercourse with the world he is aided by the most irresistible manner that ever man possessed. Such a captivating frankness, a disqualifying humility, a tenderness for all mankind, a benevolence, enlarged into universal philanthropy, which go directly to the heart. He has been accused of inordinate ambition. It would be strange indeed if one who has received so many marks of public favor, of national confidence, of popular admiration should be indifferent to praise or regardless of power. But he has not acquired his influence by servility, nor employed it in oppression. He has been throughout the firm, undeviating champion of popular liberty: and to continue so I believe is the first object of his ambition. *(Francis Walker Gilmer, Sketches of American Statesmen)*

It would be extremely difficult to trace the exact line which distinguishes these three men. It may be sometimes distinctly seen and then disappears. Mr. Jefferson's mind is the most capacious, Madison's the most rapid, Monroe's the most sure. One has most learning, another most brilliancy, a third most judgment. Mr. Jefferson surpasses in the management of bodies of men, and Monroe of individuals. We adore Mr. Jefferson, admire Mr. Madison, and esteem Mr. Monroe. *(Francis Walker Gilmer, Sketches of American Statesmen)*

Tho' not brilliant, few men were his equals in wisdom, firmness and devotion to the country. He had a wonderful intellectual patience; and could above all men, that I ever knew, when called on to decide an important point, hold the subject immovably fixed under his attention, until he had mastered it, in all of its relations. It was mainly to this admirable quality that he owed his highly accurate judgment. I have known many much more rapid in reaching the conclusion, but very few, with a certainty so unerring. . . . That I acquired & retained to the last the good opinion of one, whose name will occupy a high status in the eye of posterity, I consider among the fortunate incidents of my life. *(John C. Calhoun to Samuel Gouverneur, 8 August 1831)*

His holiness informed of your departure from Rome for the United States of America and wanting to give you a testimony of the Sovereign's acknowledgment of the services ardently rendered to the Catholic Religion by your father during his presidency of the United States, desiring that you be granted a remembrance that will recall at the same time your illustrious father and your fine reception, has seen fit to bestow upon you a cameo representing our divine savior. *(Francois Capaccini to Eliza Hay, 2 April 1834)*

Criticism of Monroe

Mr. Monroe has called upon the Secretary of State for the reasons of his recall; he seems to think that the tenure of the President's pleasure, expressed in his commission meant the pleasure of Mr. Monroe. He is trying to make a noise, and add one more puff to the bellows of faction, but his breath happens to be weak. He talks about liberty, and enlightened principles and despotism, and coalition, as much as Moliere's Tartuffe talks of piety, devotion, the love of God and sin. Mr. Pickering has answered him by plainly referring to the constitutional principles, which made an assignment of the reasons demanded improper; but at the same time gives him to understand what the reasons were, and offers in his individual character to tell him the reasons why he advised to it. This, however, Mr. Monroe chooses to decline, and the offer appears to have vexed him. He is going to publish a pamphlet; for you know with us everything ends in a pamphlet, as in France all ends in song. (John Quincy Adams to William Vans Murray, 26 October 1797)

Independently of the Manner of the Nomination & of the location of the Candidate, the Man himself is one of the Most improper & incompetent that could have been selected—Naturally dull & stupid—extremely illiterate—indecisive to a degree that would be incredible to one who did not know him—pusillanimous & of course hypocritical—has no opinion on any subject & will be always under the Govt of the worst Men—pretends as I am told, to some Knowledge of Military matters, but never commanded a platoon nor was ever fit to command one—"He served in the revolutionary War"—that is, he acted a short time as aide de Camp to ld. Stirling who was regularly drunk from Morning to Morning—Monroe's whole duty was to fill his Lordship's Tankard and hear with indications of admiration his Lordship's long stories about himself—Such is Monroes Military experience. I was with my regiment in the same division at the time—As a Lawyer, Monroe was far below Mediocrity—He never rose to the Honor of trying a Cause of the Value of an hundred pounds. This is a character exactly suited to the Views of the Virginia Junto. *(Aaron Burr to Joseph Alston, 15 November 1815)*

I consider the situation of our country inauspicious. Mr. Monroe whom I know to the Root, is much more intent on his reelection than the good of the nation—but I think the ridiculous hypocritical pageant he is now making with his sword & Cockade will, like John Q. Adams' appointment, rather prejudice than prosper his interests & views.... Monroe calculates on the Demos. & courts the feds—and is sought by both parties—in his attempt to please all he will disgust generally or I am mistaken, & will probably verify the proverb of the two Stoats. I wish he may do well, but fear the result—because he lacks Candor, truth, Independence & decision—I say so because I have experienced it.... (James Wilkinson to Henry Dearborn, 23 June 1817)

Elizabeth Kortright Monroe

[We] were at the play with [the Kortright sisters] the other evening when they made so brilliant and lovely an appearance as to depopulate all the other boxes of all the genteel male people therein. *(William Grayson to Monroe, 28 November 1785)*

[Monroe] married one of our Manhattan girls. Her name was Kortright. Her father was formerly a Merchant and lived when I was a boy, near the head of Beekmans Slip in an house since bought by Edmund Prior, in Pearl Street. There were several Sisters, that were a good deal talked of and visited when I was a stripling. Their father afterwards failed, and died very poor. But the daughters married very advantageously. One of them became the Wife of Nicholas Governeur, the late President of the Bank of New-York, and is now a Widow. Another took to husband the gentleman of whom I am writing.... She is commended exceedingly by those who know her, as a charming and amiable Woman. *(Samuel L. Mitchill to Catherine Mitchell, 11 February 1803)*

I often hear Mrs. Monroe's name mentioned with respect and admiration by the ladies of Paris. *(George Sullivan to Monroe, 5 May 1806)*

Mrs. Monroe paints very much, and has, besides, an appearance of youth which would induce a stranger to suppose her age to be thirty: in lieu of which she introduces them to her granddaughter, eighteen or nineteen years old, and to her own daughter, Mrs. Hay, of Richmond. *(Sarah Seaton diary)*

She was dressed in white and gold made in the highest style of fashion and moved not like a Queen (for that is an unpardonable word in this country) but like a goddess. *(Louisa Catherine Adams to John Adams, 1 January 1818)*

Mrs. Monroe was very elegantly dressed at the first court; her costume consisted of a white gown of India mull, embroidered with gold, her hair was braided with pearls and adorned with a lovely diadem of gold set with pearls, and ornaments of pearls adorned her throat, arms, and ears. She seemed to be between thirty and forty years old, medium sized, her face set off to advantage by her beautiful hair. *(Baron Klinkowstrom, "Letter from America," 12 February 1819)*

The other day we went to an extremely splendid state dinner at the President's House. All the foreign ministers were there. I was seated between the English and Russian ambassadors. Mrs. Monroe gave me the most flattering reception; she does the honors with much grace and dignity. She is a charming woman, much superior to the last President's wife. She is from one of the better families and received an excellent education. She spent several years in France and in England when Mr. Monroe was Ambassador. Her oldest daughter, who is married, was educated in Paris and couldn't be nicer. The younger was at school with Caroline [and] returned home last month. She was here yesterday to see Caroline. Mrs. Monroe, her daughters, and four or five other Washington women receive their clothes from Paris, but they are not in as good taste as ours. *(Rosalie Stier Calvert to Isabelle van Havre, 25 March 1819)*

The Drawing room was full tho' not crowded and we had altogether a very pleasant evening. Mrs. Monroe as usual looked beautiful. *(Louisa Catherine Adams diary, 12 January 1820)*

Wednesday evening Mrs. Monroe held a drawing room. I attended and made my bow. She was splendidly and tastily dressed, the drawing room and suit of rooms at the President's are furnished and decorated in the most splendid manner; some think too much so, but I do not; something of splendour is certainly proper about the chief magistrate, for the credit of the nation; plainness can be carried to extreme, and in national buildings and establishments, it will with good reason be styled meanness. *(Samuel F. B. Morse to Jedidiah Morse, 17 December 1820)*

…Mrs. Monroe during dinner told me that the state of her health was dreadful, the least agitation throw her into convulsions… *(Louisa Catherine Adams diary, 19 January 1821)*

I dined at the palace, and at the right hand of the Queen who was most exceedingly gracious and conversible, and I believe has no colour but what is natural, at least her colour very much increased during dinner time in the glow of occupation and attention to her guests. *(Harrison Gray Otis to Sally Otis, 27 January 1821)*

I regret that she leaves us so soon, particularly at this season, when the weather is unsettled but her desire to join you, is so great, that she cannot be induced to remain longer. *(Samuel Gouverneur to Monroe, 11 September 1825)*

This lady of whose personal attractions and accomplishments it were impossible to speak in terms of exaggeration, was, for a period a little short of half a century, the cherished affectionate partner of [Monroe's] life and fortunes. She accompanied him on all his journeying thro' this world of care, from which, by the dispensation of Providence, she had been removed only a few months before himself. The companion of his youth was the solace of his declining years, and to the close of his life enjoyed the testimonial of his affection, that with the external beauty and elegance of deportment, she united the more precious and endearing qualities which mark the fulfillment of all the social duties, and adorn with grace and fill with enjoyment, the tender relations of domestic life. *(John Quincy Adams, Eulogy for Monroe, 25 August 1831)*

Eliza Monroe Hay

Too young to profit by your instructions, I have forgotten a part of what I learned and in spite of all my pains and application I see that I have not half of the advantages which I had with you. I am reading geography, history and other studies of that kind with papa. In thinking of France, it seems to me that I would once more like to be with my charming protector where in the course of a few years I could completely finish my education; but it is useless to regret what is passed since I have to renounce the happiness of seeing you again. *(Eliza Monroe to Madame Campan, 20 June 1801)*

Eliza [was in a] plain Republican traveling dress and expressing much pleasure in their return to their native country. They think that Eliza has not at all improved in beauty but that she looks good humored and is chatty and agreeable. *(St. George Tucker to Frances Coalter, 18 December 1807)*

Mrs Monroe goes to Richmond the latter end of this month to be with her daughter at the awful period of maternity. I wish that she may go her time out, she has frequent and violent attacks of cramp in her stomach. In other respects very hearty and very happily situated. Mr Hay is one of the most tender and affectionate husbands, greatly attached to her and she to him. One of the best establishments in Virginia with flattering prospects of prosperity. In short she says that she has not a wish ungratified if her Parents were only near her. *(Elizabeth Trist to Catherine Bache, 10 July 1809)*

Eliza virtually moans over your absence. Ten times a day she repeats, if I could but see my father and dear mother here. I sometimes comfort her, and sometimes reproach her: but I do not often succeed either way: and I acknowledge that on her account as much as my own I shall rejoice, when you come beneath this roof. *(George Hay to Monroe, 12 March 1815)*

[It] is nothing with them but "my dear" and "my dear," yet do not think I have ever heard them agree on one subject since here I am, and when together they are eternally talking. As for her oracular powers, I think I heard him tell her today at dinner 3 distinct times that she "talked too much and must talk less." *(Egbert Watson, 1828, on Eliza and George Hay)*

Maria Monroe Gouverneur

[Maria] was dressed in a short frock, that reached about half way between her knees and ankles, under which she displayed a long pair of loose pantaloons, wide enough for the foot to pass through with ease, frilled round with the same stuff as her frock and pantaloons. . . . The little monkey did not fail to evince the advantages of her dress. She had a small spaniel dog with whom she was continually engaged in a trial of skill, and the general opinion seemed to be that she turned and twisted about more than the spaniel. *(St. George Tucker to Frances Coalter, 18 December 1807)*

She has gained flesh. The back of her neck is quite smooth. You cannot now see as formerly, the joints of the bone. The cold bath, in which she delights has been of great service to her. *(George Hay to Monroe, 3 July 1812)*

Maria is in perfect health, and will be, you may be assured, a most amiable and elegant young woman. She and Jane have made a formal renunciation of dolls. They were yesterday (Christmas day) presented to Hortensia as a gift. Her joy has been excessive and still continues very boisterous. *(George Hay to Monroe, 26 December 1813)*

I have heard nothing concerning [Maria Monroe's wedding] except that there were 4 Brides maids and 4 Brides men and a very handsome supper at which 42 persons sat down. *(Louisa Catherine Adams diary, 10 March 1820)*

Death of James Monroe

. . . during all May & part of June, he had chills and fever every day, they were however subdued early in June, but the distressing cough, by which he has been tormented for many years, and which was the cause of his death was too obstinate & deeply seated on his lungs to be removed by human skill. On Friday the 1st July it became evident that speedy dissolution was at hand, and he died. . . at 1/2 past three Oclock on Monday without a struggle and resigned to his fate in the most perfect possession of his mental facilities.

During his illness he often mentioned you to me, and expressed not only his most affectionate regard, respect, and esteem for you, which it gave him pleasure to say had never for forty years been for one moment interrupted, but his great regret that he should leave this world without having the happiness of once more beholding you, his oldest and most valued friend. Of Mrs. Madison he likewise often spoke with affectionate respect and esteem.

For many weeks before his death he was convinced it was impossible for him to recover, & he repeatedly expressed the most ardent wish to die; when the event approached he met it, calm and resigned. *(Tench Ringgold to James Madison, 7 July 1831)*

National Honors for James Monroe

ORDER, No. 31.

HEAD QUARTERS OF THE ARMY,
ADJUTANT GENERAL'S OFFICE
Washington, July 8th, 1831.

The General in Chief has received the following Order from the War Department:

WAR DEPARTMENT, *July 7th, 1831.*

It becomes my painful duty to announce to the Army the death of the venerated Patriot and Ex-president JAMES MONROE. This afflicting dispensation occurred on the late Anniversary of our Independence.

At a moment when a Nation of Freemen were celebrating the achievements of that devoted band of Patriots who purchased with their blood the liberty we enjoy, one of the principal actors in the great drama was called to his last account. Participating in the sensation which must fill every heart on such an afflicting occasion, and anxious to manifest his gratitude for the eminent services, and admiration for the talents and virtues of the deceased, the President directs that funeral honors be paid him at every Military Post and Station in the United States, and that the officers wear crepe on the left arm for six months.

Major General Macomb will give the necessary instructions for carrying into execution forthwith the foregoing order.

P. G. RANDOLPH,
Acting Secretary of War.

The Major General Commanding the Army, in obeying the commands of the President, in reference to the melancholy subject of the above order, cannot but indulge in those feelings which the afflicting occasion so naturally excites. The Army will sympathise with him and with their fellow citizens generally, in the loss which the country has sustained in the death of Ex-president MONROE. His public services in the field and in the cabinet, are too well known to require a recital here. Suffice it to say, that he was an ornament to the American Nation, both as a Soldier and a Statesman—constant in the dissemination of those principles which led to the achievement of the glorious Independence of these States, and ever ready to defend them at every hazard. An example worthy of the contemplation of every American citizen.

On the first Monday after the arrival of this order at each Military Post, the troops will be paraded at 10 o'clock A. M. and the order read to them, after which, all labors for the day will cease.

The National flag will be displayed at half staff.

At dawn of day, 13 guns will be fired, and afterwards at intervals of thirty minutes between the rising and setting sun, a single gun will be fired; and at the close of the day, a salute of 24 guns.

The colours of the several Regiments will be put in mourning for the space of six months, and the officers will wear crepe during the same period.

By order of ALEXANDER MACOMB, Maj. Gen. Commanding U. S. Army.

R. Jones
Adj. Gen.

Index

Adams, Abigail—78
Adams, John Quincy—16, 48, 67, 85; JM on—31; on JM—82, 85
Adams, Louisa Catherine—83, 84,87
Advice to youth—20, 23, 24-26
Affection for family—19-21, 76-77
American Revolution, JM in—11, 30-31, 72, 79; JM on—51-53, 82
Ash Lawn—See Highland
Attorney, JM as—11, 16, 23, 27, 34, 82
Baring, Francis—46
Blow, Robert—79
Breckinridge, John—67
Brown, James—20
Bunker Hill—52
Burke, Frances Maury—45
Burr, Aaron—82
Butler, Pierce—77
Calhoun, John C.—81
Calvert, Caroline—84
Calvert, Rosalie Stier—84
Campan, Jeanne-Louise-Henriette—85
Campbell, George W—19
Canuson, S.—47
Capaccini, Francois—81
Cardelli, Pietro—46
Civic Virtue—51-55, 59, 61
Clay, Henry—68
College of William & Mary—11, 34, 35, 59, 73-74
Dawson, John—73
Duponceau, Pierre—36

Education, JM's—11, 17, 27, 33-35, 80; JM on—23, 25-26, 59-62
Everett, Charles—40, 58
Farming—37-39, 77
Federalists—55, 66
France, JM as U. S. minister to—12, 31-32, 66-67, 76-77, 81-82, 84; Revolution—17, 31-32
Franklin, William Temple—73
Gates, Guerdon—78
Gilmer, Francis Walker—80
Gouverneur, Maria Hester Monroe (daughter)—12, 15, 19, 20, 48, 84; JM on—21-22, 46; education—21; description—86-87; portrait—46, 48
Gouverneur, Samuel (son-in-law)—15, 19-21, 48, 85; portrait—48
Grayson, William—83
Great Britain—66-68; JM as U. S. minister to—12, 19, 77, 84
Greece—69-70
Hamilton, Alexander—72
Harvard College—61
Hay, Eliza Monroe (daughter)—11, 15, 43, 81, 83, 84; JM on—20-21, 46-47; description—85-86; education—85; portrait—46-47
Hay, George (son-in-law)—15, 20, 21, 47, 86-87; portrait—47
Hay, Hortensia (granddaughter)—15, 20, 21, 83, 87
Highland—12, 39, 50; view—50; residence at—27, 38, 40; construction—38-39, 50
Indians, integration into American society—63, 64, 79; education of—63-64, 79; removal—63-64
Jefferson, Thomas—11, 16, 22, 38, 76, 77, 80; JM on—27-30; JM to—23, 29, 33, 34, 38-40, 46, 49, 55-57, 59, 62, 66, 67, 69; on JM—73-74, 77, 79; death—28-29
Jones, Joseph (uncle)—16, 19, 22, 38; JM on—26-27
Jones, William—63
Kirkland, John—61
Klinkowstrom, Baron—84
Lafayette, Madame—17, 31-32
Lafayette, Marquis—17, 32, 40
Laurens, John—72
Lee, Charles—72
Lewis, Nicholas—20

Libraries—34, 79
Louisiana Purchase—12, 66-67
Macomb, Alexander—90
Madison, Bishop James—74
Madison, Dolley—39, 45, 90
Madison, James—12, 16, 73-74, 79-80, 90; JM on—29-30; JM to—22, 27, 38-39, 66-67
Mason, George—17, 33
Mason, John—59
Mason, Stevens T.—67
Massachusetts Society of the Cincinnati—52
McLean, John—31
Mercer, Charles F.—19
Mercer, John F.—36
Missouri Compromise—69
Mitchell, Stephen, M.—44
Mitchill, Samuel L.—77, 83
Monroe Doctrine—13, 71
Monroe, Andrew—15, 24; JM on—24, 49; portrait—49
Monroe, Elizabeth (wife)—11, 13, 15, 22, 39, 46, 76-77, 86; JM on—19-20, 44; description—15, 45, 83-85; portrait—44-45; health—15, 19, 20, 21, 84; death—13, 20
Monroe, Elizabeth Jones (mother)—16, 26
Monroe, Eliza—see Hay
Monroe, Emily (niece)—16, 23-24
Monroe, James, description of—42, 72-81; criticism of—81-82; health—19, 29, 40, 41, 88; portrait—42-43; death—13, 88-90
Monroe, James Jr. (nephew)—15-16, 24, 35, 49; JM on—25-26
Monroe, James Spence (son)—12, 15, 22
Monroe, Joseph Jones (brother)—15; JM on—23-24, 49; portrait—49
Monroe, Maria Hester—See Gouverneur
Monroe, Spence (father)—16, 26
Montgomery, Janet—22
Montgomery, Richard—22
Montlezun, Baron—78
Morse, Samuel F. B.—43, 84
Nashville (TN) Female Academy—61

National defense—62-63, 65-66
New York City residence—40
Nicholas, Wilson C.—67
Oak Hill—13, 40-41
Otis, Harrison Gray—85
Parker, Daniel—35
Peale, Raphaelle—44
Perry, Oliver Hazard—17, 33
Pickering, Timothy—81
Pinckney, Thomas—58
Plumer, William—77
President, JM as—12, 16, 31, 55, 65-66, 78-82
President's House—84
Presidential election, 1808—12, 29
Prevost, Theodosia—35
Randolph, Martha Jefferson—28
Randolph, Philip G.—89
Religion—22, 36, 61, 81
Retirement—13, 20, 39-40
Ringgold, Tench—88
Romance—35-36
Seaton, Sarah—83
Secretary of State, JM as—12, 34-35
Sené, Louis—44
Short, William—17, 32-33, 37, 73
Skipwith, Fulwar—21, 37, 39, 47
Slave trade, suppression of—57-59
Slavery—57-59
Slaves, colonization of—57-58; treatment of—58; emancipation—59
Smith, Larkin—54
Smith, Margaret Bayard—45
Spain, JM as U. S. minister to—12
Spanish American independence—70-71
Stuart, Gilbert—42-43
Sullivan, George—83
Swann, Thomas—20
Taylor, John—77
Thayer, Sylvanus—62

Thompson, Cephas—47
Trist, Elizabeth—21, 47, 86
Tucker, St. George—59, 86-87
Tyler, John—28
U. S. Congress, messages to—31-35, 55-56, 59, 64-66, 70-71
U. S. Constitution, ratification of—12, 30
Union of the states—53-55, 69
University of Virginia—61-62
Vanderlyn, John—45
Vaughan, Sarah—73
Virginia General Assembly, message to—28, 51-54, 60, 62
Virginia, JM as governor of—12, 74-76
War of 1812—17, 33, 67-69
Washington College (Washington, PA)—61
Washington, George—16; JM on—29-31
Watson, Egbert—79, 86
Westmoreland County farm—11, 37-38
Wilberforce, William—58
Wilkinson, James—82
Windsor (VT) Female Academy—61
Wirt, William—76
Women, education of—61
Wood, James—73
Woodford, William—34

Quotations of James Monroe